the practical
woodwork book

GW00541357

the practical woodwork book

Anthony Hontoir

Drawings and photographs by the author

John Murray

© Anthony Hontoir 1986

First published 1986 by
John Murray (Publishers) Ltd
50 Albemarle Street, London W1X 4BD

Typeset by Leaper and Gard, Bristol
Printed and Bound in Great Britain by Clark Constable Ltd, Edinburgh

British Library Cataloguing in Publication Data

Hontoir, Anthony
    The practical woodwork book.
    1. Woodwork
    I. Title
    684'.08   TT185
    ISBN 0-7195-4242-1

contents

Preface   vi

how to make the joints

1   The butt joint   2
2   The dowelled joint   2
3   The housing joint   3
4   The mitre joint   3
5   The halved joint   3
6   The through mortise and tenon joint   5
7   The stopped mortise and tenon joint   7
8   The bridle joint   9
9   The dovetail joint   10

the projects

1   The ship   14
2   The gun   18
3   The egg-rack   22
4   The teapot stand   25
5   The kitchen-roll holder   28
6   The dog box   31
7   The box calendar   35
8   The picnic table   40
9   The lighthouse   45
10   The garden chair   49
11   The table tennis table   55
12   The bathroom cabinet   60
13   The bedside cabinet   64
14   The three coffee tables   70
15   The passageway door   76
16   The driveway gates   81

Tool list   88
Tool and materials manufacturers and
suppliers   90

preface

This book aims to give a varied range of woodwork projects for use in schools and adult evening classes.

Starting with a short section which describes how to make all the major joints, the book carries on with the main section of projects. The first of these are simple toys that give the beginner useful exercises in cutting many of the joints, then the projects gradually increase in difficulty so that towards the end of the book the woodwork pupil is tackling furniture and joinery. A high standard of work is required at this level.

The various woods used in the projects must not be regarded as the only types that are suitable, and alternatives are always mentioned, where appropriate. The pupil is advised to think very carefully about the choice of material, whether it is softwood or hardwood; cheap and freely available, or rare and relatively expensive. It would be impossible to list all the reasonable alternatives in these pages, partly because the availability of certain woods changes from one year to the next.

There are several different types of wood glue that you can use, but the choice is essentially between a P.V.A. adhesive which is already mixed and comes in a plastic dispenser bottle, or the resin powder which must always be freshly mixed with a measured quantity of water. Generally, the best adhesives are those that are slow to set, and therefore the work must be held tightly together with clamps for perhaps a day or so.

The author would like to express his grateful thanks to a number of people in preparing this book.

Firstly, to Dean Stiles and Christine Doyle, former editors of the magazine *Popular DIY* in which all the projects in this book originally appeared with the exception of the ship, gun, egg-rack and lighthouse.

In planning the format of the book, together with deciding which projects to include or omit, which projects to write specially for it, and for the numerous points of detail, the author is indebted to Glen Wilbraham, woodwork master at Porthcawl Comprehensive School, Mid Glamorgan, and also to several of his pupils who made useful comments and observations.

Thanks are also due to Steven Jones, for his many words of advice, particularly on the joinery.

Not least, grateful acknowledgement is made to Richard Stewart for reading the material in the early stages and putting forward a number of helpful suggestions.

A.H.

how to make the joints

how to make the joints

1 the butt joint

The butt joint is formed between the squared edges or the sides of the two pieces, or the edge of one and the side of the other.

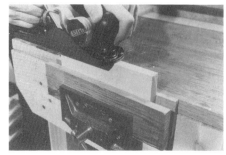

1.1 Cut and plane the wood to the required size.

1.2 Apply glue to the joint.

1.3 If desired, strengthen the joint with nails or panel pins.

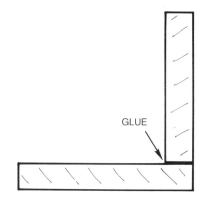

GLUE

1.4 Hold the two pieces of wood in contact with clamps while the glue dries and hardens.

2 the dowelled joint

The dowelled joint can take several forms, but it is generally like the butt joint, fastened together by lengths of dowelling.

2.1 Cut and plane the wood to the required size.

2.2 Drill dowel holes in the face side and face edge of the two lengths to be joined, drilling to a measured depth. The drill diameter should equal that of the dowel.

2.3 Cut the dowelling to length and make a saw-cut along it for the glue to squeeze out during assembly. Twist the ends in a pencil-sharpener once or twice to round them off and make for an easier fit in the dowel holes.

SAW-CUT

DOWEL

2.4 Apply glue to the dowelling and the holes. Place the dowels in position and tap the joint together with the mallet.

3 the housing joint

The housing joint is formed by fitting the edge of one piece into a groove cut along the length, or across the grain, of the second piece.

3.1 Cut and plane the wood to the required size.

3.2 Cut a groove in the face side of one piece with the plough plane, equal in width to the thickness of the piece to be joined. The depth of the groove

should be half the thickness of the piece, or less.

3.3 Apply glue to the groove and tap the joint together with the mallet.

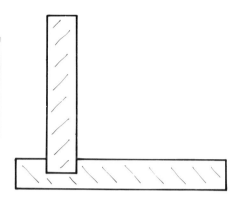

4 the mitre joint

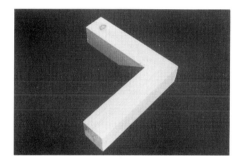

The mitre joint is formed by each of the two pieces being cut at the end at an angle of 45° and joined together at right-angles. Sometimes the angle is varied to suit different types of work.

4.1 Place the first piece in the mitre box and cut an angle of 45° with the tenon saw.

4.2 Cut a corresponding angle in the second piece to make an overall right-angle, or 90°.

4.3 Glue the two pieces together.

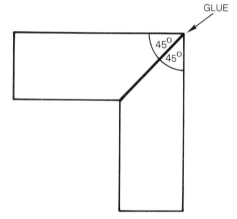

4.4 The mitre joint is often reinforced with nails, dowelling or thin 'keys' — narrow strips of scrap wood notched into the joint to give it strength.

5 the halved joint

The halved joint is used to join two lengths of wood, usually at right-angles. The joint may be located either along the length of the wood, or at the end of it. Our illustrated example shows both kinds.

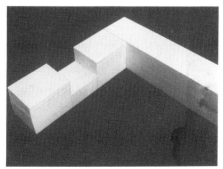

5.1 Measure and mark the width of the wood on the face of the first piece in the required position along its length, squaring all around.

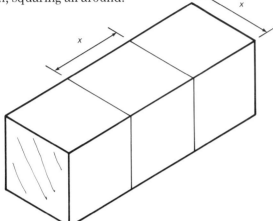

5.2 Mark in the depth of the joint, which is equal to half the thickness of the wood, using the marking gauge set to that distance.

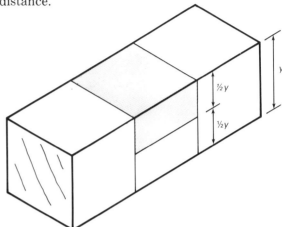

5.3 Saw down the sides of the joint with the tenon saw, cutting on the waste side of the two lines. Make a series of additional saw-cuts between these lines. Stop sawing when you reach the depth line.

5.4 Chisel out the waste, working first from one side, then from the other, removing a little at a time. As you approach the depth line, pare off the waste with a slicing action of the chisel.

5.5 Measure and mark the width of the wood at the end of the second piece, squaring all around. Use the marking gauge at the same setting to scribe the depth line, marking it on the two sides and the end.

5.6 Remove the waste with the tenon saw only, placing the piece upright in the vice and sawing on the

waste side of the line. Place it lengthways in the vice to saw off the shoulder.

5.7 Fit the two parts of the joint together and assemble with glue. The joint may be strengthened by screwing together.

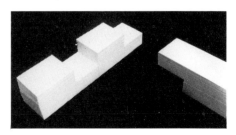

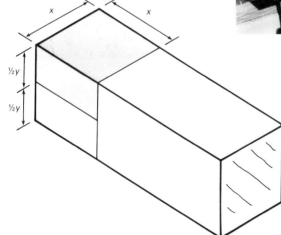

6 the through mortise and tenon joint

The mortise and tenon joint is one of the most common joints to be used in woodwork. It consists of a mortise, or hole, cut into one piece of wood, and a tenon, or tongue, equal in size to the mortise, cut in the second piece. The tenon fits exactly into the mortise, and joins the two pieces together at right-angles. Both the mortise and the tenon are equal in width to one-third the thickness of the wood. Our example is a two-shouldered through mortise and tenon: as its name implies, the mortise passes through the entire width of the wood, and may be secured with wedges.

6.1 Measure and mark in the mortise. As this is a two-shouldered mortise, its length is equal to the width of the wood. Mark in the position of the mortise, squaring pencil lines right around the piece.

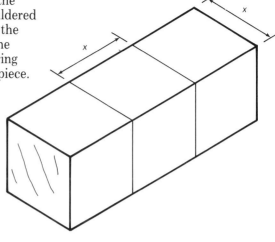

6.2 Set the pointers of the mortise gauge to one-third the thickness of the wood and adjust the fence of the gauge so that the pointers mark the wood centrally. Scribe lines on both edges of the piece, marking them between the lines already drawn. You now have rectangular spaces marked on opposite faces of the wood.

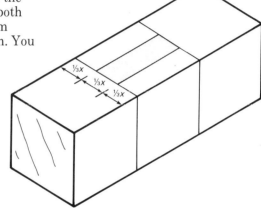

6.3 Place the piece in the vice and drill a series of holes in the mortise area to remove most of the waste quickly and easily, using a twist drill or centre bit that is slightly smaller in diameter than the width of the mortise. Drill halfway through the wood, then turn the piece over and repeat the drilling from the opposite side, so that the holes pass right through the mortise.

6.4 Remove the remaining waste with the chisel and mallet, working the chisel from the centre of the mortise gradually towards one end, then the other. Cut the ends cleanly with a vertical chop from the chisel.

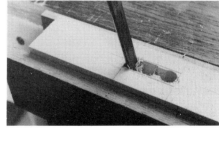

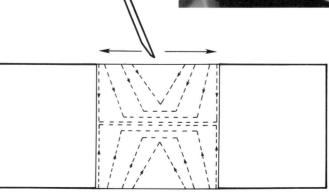

6.5 Measure and mark the tenon. The length of the tenon is equal to the width of the wood. Mark in the shoulder lines at the end of the piece, squaring right around the wood. With the mortise gauge set as before, mark in the two parallel tenon lines, scribing them on the top and bottom edges and the end of the piece.

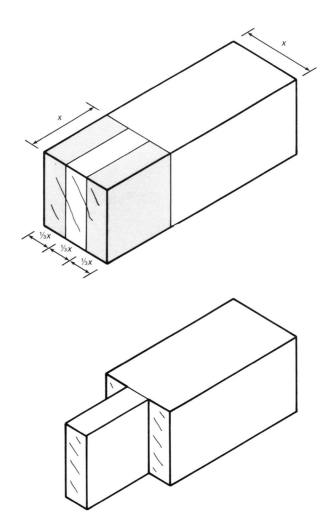

6.6 Place the wood at an angle in the vice, and saw down the lines with the tenon saw, cutting on the waste side. When you reach the shoulder line, reverse the piece in the vice and repeat the cut. Then place the wood upright and complete the two parallel saw-cuts down to the shoulder line. Lay the piece lengthways in the vice and saw down the shoulder lines to remove the waste.

6.7 File the mortise and tenon smooth, and tap the tenon into the mortise gently with the mallet. When it fits fully home without binding, the joint may then be fixed permanently together with glue.

6.8 To secure the mortise more firmly with wedges, measure the mortise deliberately extra-long on the outside edge and chisel out two sloping portions within the mortise, working them approximately halfway through. Cut triangular hardwood wedges to fit, then glue these in and tap them home when the joint is assembled.

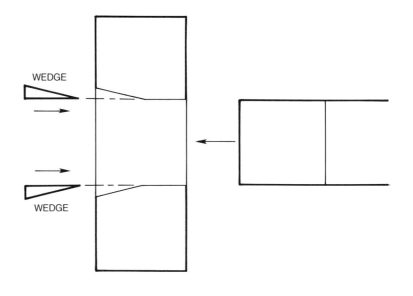

7 the stopped mortise and tenon joint

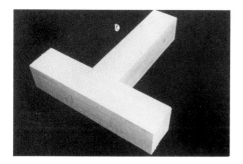

This is a slightly different mortise and tenon from the previous example, though in general principle it is the same. The differences are that the mortise is stopped, in other words it does not pass right through the width of the wood but is cut three-quarters of the way through, and the tenon is four-shouldered. The joint may be secured by draw-boring.

7.1 Measure and mark in the mortise. As this is a four-shouldered mortise and tenon, the length of the mortise is less than the width of the wood. But start by marking in the full width, squaring pencil lines right around the piece.

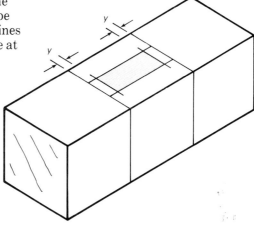

7.2 Set the pointers of the mortise gauge to one-third the thickness of the wood and adjust the fence of the gauge so that the pointers mark the wood centrally. Scribe lines on the one edge where the mortise is to be cut, marking them between the lines already drawn. Set in the mortise at either end by a pre-determined amount, equal to the width of the second pair of tenon shoulders.

7.3 Place the piece in the vice and drill a series of holes in the mortise area to remove most of the waste quickly and easily, using a twist drill or centre bit that is slightly smaller in diameter than the width of the mortise. Drill to a depth not exceeding three-quarters the width of the wood, using a depth-gauge to check.

7.4 Remove the remaining waste with the chisel and mallet, working the chisel from the centre of the mortise gradually towards one end, then the other. Cut the ends cleanly with a vertical chop from the chisel. For fine work, as with small mortises, do not use the drill method but chop out all the waste with the chisel.

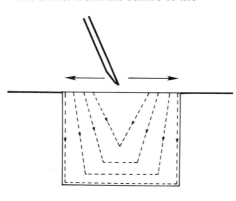

7.5 Measure and mark the tenon. The length of the tenon is equal to three-quarters the width of the wood. Mark in the shoulder lines at the end of the piece, squaring right around the wood. With the mortise gauge set as before, mark in the two parallel tenon lines, scribing them on the top and bottom edges and the end of the piece.

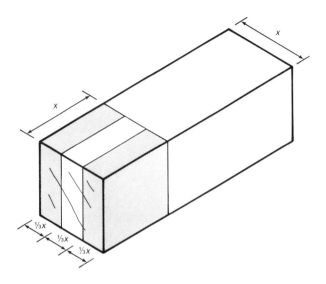

7.6 Place the wood at an angle in the vice, and saw down the lines with the tenon saw, cutting on the waste side. When you reach the shoulder line, reverse the piece in the vice and repeat the cut. Then place the wood upright, and complete the two parallel saw-cuts down to the shoulder line. Lay the piece lengthways in the vice and saw down the shoulder lines to remove the waste.

7.7 Measure in the second pair of shoulders, equal to the amount by which the mortise was set in, and saw these off. File the mortise and tenon smooth, and tap the tenon into the mortise gently with the mallet. When it fits fully home without binding, the joint may then be fixed permanently together with glue.

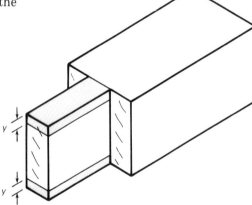

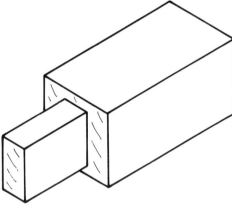

7.8 To secure the stopped mortise and tenon more firmly, use the draw-boring technique. This involves drilling a small-diameter hole centrally through the side of the mortise, and drilling the same hole through the tenon in a slightly offset position. When a dowel or screw is driven through the hole during assembly, it will pull the tenon tightly into the mortise. It is usual to countersink the hole when screwing home.

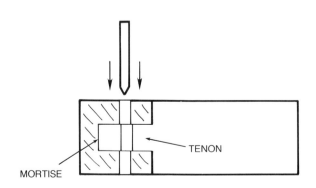

TENON

MORTISE

8 the bridle joint

The bridle joint is the opposite of the through mortise and tenon. Two shoulders are cut away from one piece at the point along its length where the joint is required, and a receiver slot cut in the other piece so that the two parts fit together at right-angles. As with the mortise and tenon, the slot is equal to one-third the thickness of the wood.

8.1 Measure and mark the position of the two shoulders in the first piece. The procedure is exactly the same as for marking a through mortise. The width of the wood is marked on one face, and squared right around.

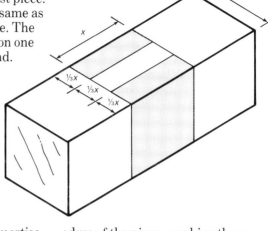

8.2 Set the pointers of the mortise gauge to one-third the thickness of the wood and adjust the fence of the gauge so that the pointers mark the wood centrally. Scribe lines on both edges of the piece, marking them between the lines already drawn. You now have rectangular spaces marked on opposite faces of the wood.

8.3 Remove the two outer shoulders, leaving the portion in the middle. As with the halved joint, cut away the waste with the tenon saw

and the chisel, working the saw on the waste side of the shoulder lines. Chisel off the waste, finishing the work with a slicing action to give a smooth flat surface to the portion left in the middle.

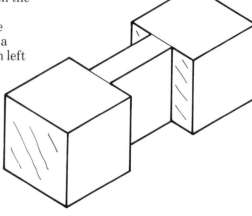

8.4 Measure and mark the slot in the end of the second piece. The marking procedure is the same as for the tenon. The depth of the slot is equal to the width of the wood. Mark in the depth lines at the end of the

piece, squaring right around the wood. With the mortise gauge set as before, mark in the two parallel slot lines, scribing them on the top and bottom edges and the end of the piece.

8.5 Place the wood at an angle in the vice, and saw down the lines with the tenon saw, cutting on the waste side. When you reach the depth line, reverse the piece in the vice and repeat the cut. Then place the wood upright, and complete the two parallel saw-cuts down to the depth line.

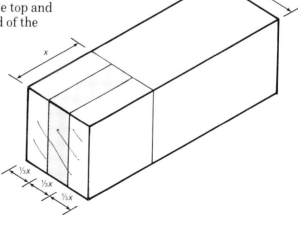

8.6 Lay the piece lengthways in the vice and chisel out the slot, working the chisel halfway through from one side, then turning the piece over to complete the chiselling from the other side. Finally chop vertically downwards on the depth line and clean up the inside surfaces of the slot.

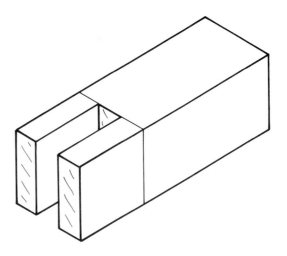

8.7 File both parts of the joint smooth, and fit them together, tapping gently with the mallet. If there is resistance, file down the part that binds, until the joint fits easily.

8.8 Apply glue to both parts of the joint and knock it fully together.

9 the dovetail joint

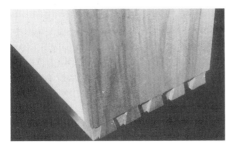

The dovetail joint possesses great strength, and has a wide number of applications, so it is an important joint to learn. The two parts are joined in such a way that the assembled joint cannot be pulled apart in one direction, due to the wedge shape of the dovetail which is housed in the receiver socket.

9.1 Measure and cut the two pieces to be joined, and plane the ends square. Measure accurately the thickness of the wood, and mark a line the distance of this measurement from the end of each piece, squaring all around.

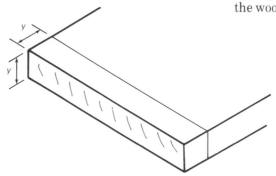

9.2 Mark in the dovetails on the first piece with the pencil. These are marked at a particular angle, and it is a good idea to make a card template cut to that angle which will ensure consistent results throughout. The number of dovetails per joint is usually determined by the width of the wood — our example has five.

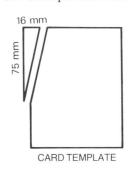

16 mm

75 mm

CARD TEMPLATE

9.3 There is no rigid formula to stick to, but for guidance remember that the narrowest part of the dovetail should be sufficiently wide to maintain its strength and prevent it from snapping off. The width of each dovetail at its narrowest point is equal to the distance by which it is separated from its neighbour, denoted x in the diagram. Set in the end dovetails by half of this amount from each edge, denoted $\frac{1}{2}x$.

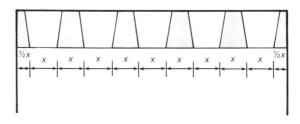

9.4 Using the template, mark in the slopes of the dovetails. With the square, complete the marking by pencilling in the lines on the end-grain.

9.5 Clamp the piece upright in the vice and saw on the waste side of the lines with the tenon saw, taking each saw-cut down as far as the shoulder line.

9.6 Transfer the dovetail positions to the receiver piece to show where the slots are to be cut. This is done by placing the receiver piece upright in the vice and holding the dovetailed piece accurately in position at right-angles to it. Draw the tenon saw carefully through each kerf to make a mark.

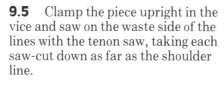

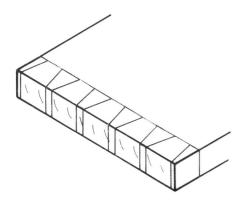

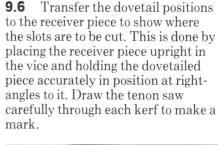

9.7 Use the square and pencil to mark in lines that join the saw-cuts up to the shoulder lines, and then saw down to the shoulders working the saw once again on the waste side of the original marking.

9.8 Chop out the waste between the slots and the dovetails using the bevel chisel and mallet. Starting with the dovetailed piece, use the chisel to remove the wedge-shaped waste portions. The bevel chisel must be used because the bevels match the slopes of the dovetails and the chisel does not damage the wood.

9.9 Work the chisel with care, starting fractionally short of the shoulder line, holding the chisel perpendicular to the face of the wood so that the blade cuts straight down into it. Then bring the chisel back to the shoulder line and chop down until the blade passes halfway through the piece. Turn it over and cut from the other side, and remove the waste. Saw off the two narrower waste portions at the edges.

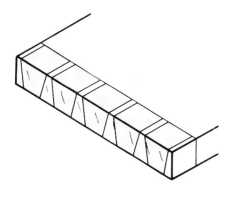

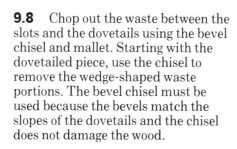

9.10 Chop out the waste between the slots in the second piece using a similar method, firstly holding the chisel vertically (shown), then working it at an angle to match the slope of the dovetails.

9.11 Unlike other types of joint, the dovetail must not be fitted experimentally into its housing to check that it fits well, because it will be difficult to separate the two parts of the joint again without loosening or splitting them. The most you can do is hold them together at the point of entry to see how far they appear to agree or disagree. Pare away any parts that are likely to bind.

9.12 Apply glue to both parts of the joint and tap together with the mallet.

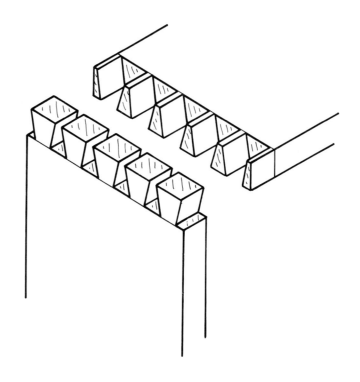

the projects

project 1
the ship

The model ship is a cargo
steamer. It is an easy toy to
make, and if you paint and
varnish it, you will find that it
can be floated on water to give
a realistic impression.

FIGURE 1.1

how it is designed

The ship is purposely designed to give
useful practice in cutting various
types of joint, as described in greater
detail in Section 1 of the book.

For instance, the bow of the ship,
or the front end, consists of two mitre
cuts; the no. 1 and no. 2 cargo holds
are derived from halved joints; the
stern, or the rear end, is a semi-
circular rounded and carved portion;
and the funnel is one example of a
dowelled joint, where the dowel hole
is drilled at right-angles to the grain.

Certain small finishing details such
as the cutting out of the bridge, the
removal of excess wood from the
forecastle at the bow and the
sterncastle at the stern, the fixing of
two masts, may be left to individual
choice, though they are fully
described in the instructions.

The wood used is red deal, but
other softwoods like pine or Parana
pine are equally suitable.

tool list

Pencil	marking gauge	mallet	mitre box
ruler	tenon saw	handbrace with	bradawl
square	hacksaw	16 mm centre bit	file
compasses	19 mm bevel chisel	plane	trimming knife

cutting list

Item	Long mm	Wide mm	Thick mm
1 block of softwood	240	48	48
	Long mm	Diameter mm	
Dowelling for funnel	30	16	
Wooden cocktail sticks for masts	50	2	

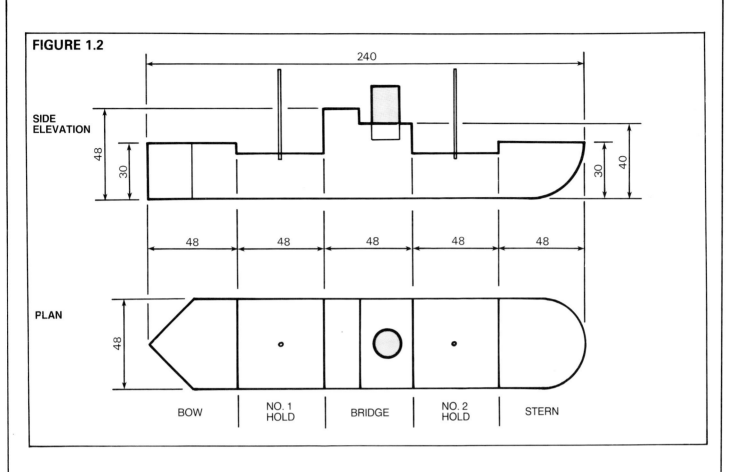

FIGURE 1.2

SIDE ELEVATION

240

48

30

30

40

48   48   48   48   48

PLAN

48

BOW   NO. 1 HOLD   BRIDGE   NO. 2 HOLD   STERN

how to make it

1   Cut and plane the block of softwood to size.

2   Divide the block up into five equal sections along its length using the pencil and ruler, each section being 48 mm long. Square right around the block at each of these points. The five sections are for the bow, no. 1 cargo hold, bridge, no. 2 cargo hold and stern (Figure 1.2).

3   Measure and mark for the mitres in the bow section. Set the marking gauge to mark midway along the wood, a distance of 24 mm. Run the pointer of the gauge on both the top and bottom faces in such a way that each line divides the front section in half along its length. Then join these two lines with a single vertical line on the end-grain (Figure 1.3) to form the apex of the mitres.

4   Place the block in the mitre box and cut the mitres with the tenon

saw. The waste is shown by the shaded areas in Figure 1.3. The kerf of the saw should produce a perfect point at the bow.

5   The next step is to make the two halved joints for the two cargo holds. These are both cut in exactly the

same way. With the marking gauge set as before, mark each halved joint by running the pointer firstly along one side of the block between the appropriate pencil lines. Then turn the block around and scribe the other side likewise.

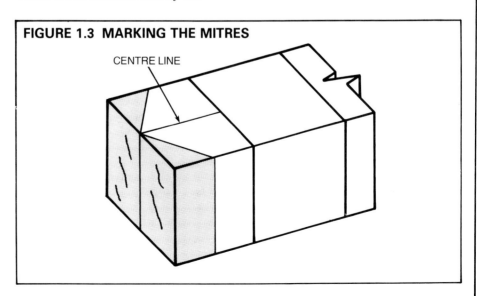

FIGURE 1.3   MARKING THE MITRES

CENTRE LINE

15

FIGURE 1.4

6   Clamp the block in the vice with the top face uppermost and saw down to the scribed depth line (Figure 1.4). Chisel out the waste using the 19 mm chisel and the mallet, applying the usual method of cutting a halved joint. Finish off by filing smooth the cargo holds.

7   Mark the semi-circular stern. Set a pair of geometrical compasses to a radius of 24 mm and place the point at the centre of the rearmost section's top face. Draw in a semi-circle to depict the stern of the ship (Figure 1.5). Turn the block upside down and make the same compass marking on the bottom face.

8   Remove the waste in small pieces with the hacksaw, keeping always to the waste side of the curved lines. Complete the rounding off of the stern by clamping the piece sideways in the vice and planing down the rough hacksaw work.

9   Turn the wood upside down in the vice and carve a rounded end at the stern as shown in the side elevation of Figure 1.2, finishing with medium- and then fine-grade sandpaper.

10   Trim 18 mm from the top of both the forecastle and the sterncastle, removing the waste with the tenon saw. By taking off this amount to leave a height of 30 mm, the ship will look more realistic.

11   Mark out and remove a rectangular portion measuring 28 mm by 48 mm by 8 mm (Figure 1.6) from the top of the centre section to create a bridge.

12   The funnel fits in the recess that this makes behind the bridge. It is cut from 16 mm diameter dowelling, a length of 30 mm being ample. Mark a

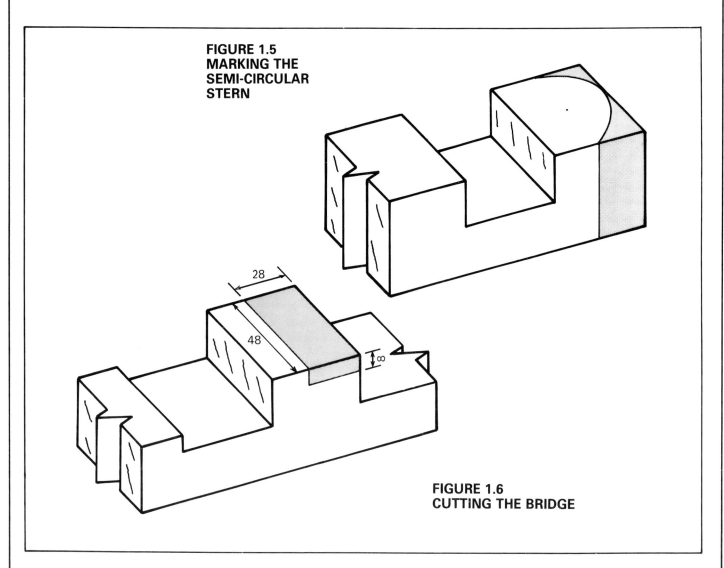

**FIGURE 1.5
MARKING THE
SEMI-CIRCULAR
STERN**

28

48

8

**FIGURE 1.6
CUTTING THE BRIDGE**

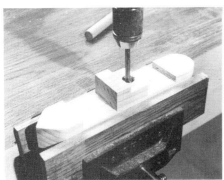

FIGURE 1.7

point at the centre of the recess with the bradawl and drill a hole 10 mm deep using the handbrace fitted with the 16 mm centre bit (Figure 1.7).

13 The two masts can be cut from wooden cocktail sticks, removing the pointed ends with the trimming knife. Make the holes for these in the centre of the holds with the bradawl.

14 Sandpaper all the surfaces of the ship thoroughly to erase pencil marks and round off the edges of the hull.

15 Mix a small quantity of wood glue and stick the funnel and masts in position, placing the assembly to one side until the glue has set hard.

16 Paint the ship. You could use various colour schemes: for example, white, red and dark grey. Finally give the surfaces a coating with clear varnish.

questions

(a) Why use a softwood and not a hardwood for this project?

(b) In marking out the five sections along the block (Paragraph 2), what special precaution must you take when using the square?

(c) Paragraph 4 tells you to use the mitre box to prepare the two mitres. What problems would you expect to encounter when using the mitre box, and how do you get over these?

(d) Paragraph 16 tells you to cut a 30 mm length of dowelling for the ship's funnel. How would you suggest marking a perfect pencil line right around the dowelling?

exercises

(i) Prepare two three-dimensional drawings of the ship, one viewed from the bow quarter, the other from the stern quarter.

(ii) You may have a favourite type of ship, like an ocean-going cruise liner, a naval frigate, or a smaller boat like a yacht or motor cruiser. Adapt this simple design to a ship or boat of your own choice, varying the proportions and location of the major features.

project 2
the gun

The model gun is a typical example of a light sub-machine gun, having a long breech, short barrel, a shaped handgrip butt, magazine clip mounted on the left-hand side, and a gunsight on the top.

how it is designed

The main object of the gun is to give further practice in cutting some of the common joints to be found in woodwork.

The magazine is mounted to the breech with a through mortise and tenon joint, the tenon having two shoulders; the sight is a stopped mortise and tenon, the tenon in this case having four shoulders; the butt is fitted using the bridle joint, and the gun barrel is another type of dowelled joint, different from the one in Project 1 because the dowel hole is drilled into the end-grain.

Use a softwood, like red deal or pine.

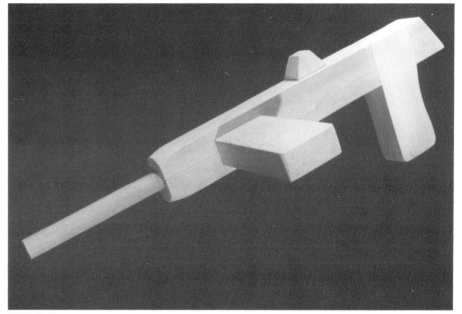

FIGURE 2.1

tool list

Pencil
ruler
square
mortise gauge
tenon saw
hacksaw
6 mm bevel chisel
19 mm bevel chisel
mallet
handbrace with 16 mm centre bit
plane
spokeshave
file

cutting list

Item	Long mm	Wide mm	Thick mm
1 breech	300	38	28
1 butt	120	44	28
1 magazine	130	46	22
1 sight	30	32	22

	Long mm	Diameter mm
1 barrel	140	16

Note: The grain runs along the length of each piece.

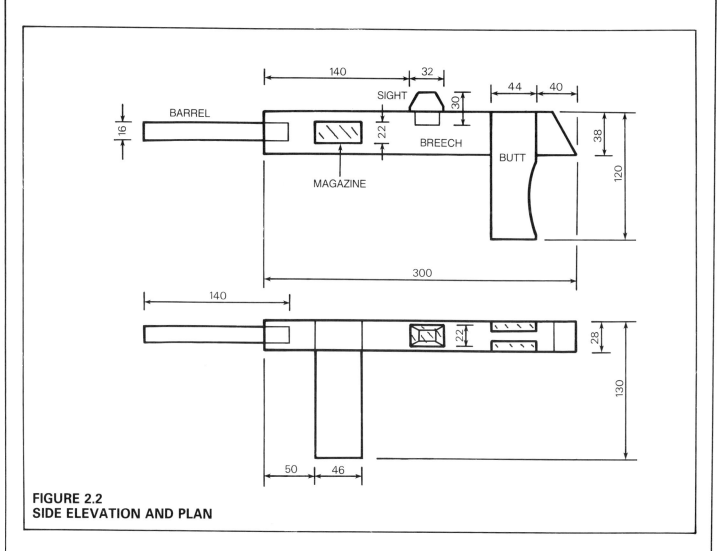

FIGURE 2.2
SIDE ELEVATION AND PLAN

how to make it

1 Measure and cut the breech to length, planing it to the required size. Repeat the same process for the butt, magazine and sight.

2 Begin by fitting the magazine to the left side of the breech using the through mortise and tenon joint (Figure 2.3). Mark in the position of the mortise (Figure 2.2), squaring the lines right around the wood.

3 Set the pointers of the mortise gauge to 7mm, which is one-third the thickness of the magazine, and adjust the fence so that the gauge marks the side face of the breech centrally. Score parallel lines between the pencil lines on both sides.

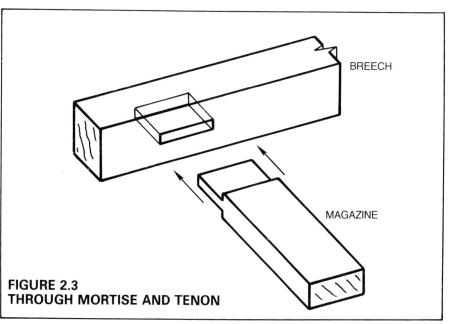

FIGURE 2.3
THROUGH MORTISE AND TENON

4 Clamp the wood securely in the vice and chop out the mortise with the 6 mm chisel, starting at the centre of the marked-out area and working outwards.

5 When you have cut approximately halfway through the thickness of the wood, turn the piece over in the vice and start chopping out the mortise from the other side until the chisel breaks through. Clean up the mortise and file it smooth.

6 Mark out the tenon at one end of the magazine, and remove the two shoulders using the tenon saw. File the shoulders smooth and fit the tenon into the mortise. If it refuses to tap in easily with the mallet, do not force it but enlarge the mortise slightly and file the tenon again until the two parts fit with gentle pressure. Dismantle the joint and place the magazine to one side.

7 Mark and cut the mortise and tenon for the gunsight, which is mounted on top of the breech. This is different from the previous joint: it is cut to a depth of 13 mm, and the tenon is four-shouldered (Figure 2.4). The sight itself may be shaped like a flat-topped pyramid, using the hacksaw and plane.

8 The next step is to fit the butt to the breech, using the bridle joint (Figure 2.5). Like the mortise and tenon, this should be measured and marked with the mortise gauge set to one-third the thickness of both pieces.

9 Firstly, cut the shoulders off the breech, using the tenon saw to make a row of saw-cuts and then chiselling these away with the 19 mm chisel. Cut the slot from the butt with the saw and the 6 mm chisel, and fit the two parts together.

10 The rear edge of the butt is shaped below the line of the slot with a shallow curve. This is marked in with the pencil. Clamp the piece in the vice and shape the curve with the spokeshave, working it from both directions towards the centre of the curve (Figure 2.6).

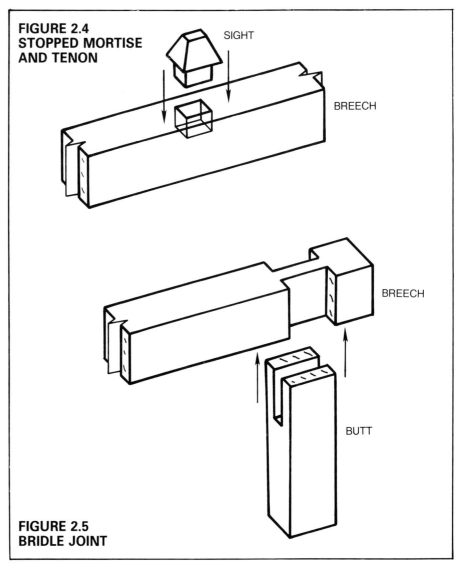

**FIGURE 2.4
STOPPED MORTISE
AND TENON**

SIGHT

BREECH

BREECH

BUTT

**FIGURE 2.5
BRIDLE JOINT**

11 Cut a 140 mm length of dowelling for the barrel. Mark the centre of the front end of the breech and place the wood vertically in the vice. Drill a hole straight into the end-grain using the handbrace with the 16 mm centre bit, drilling to a depth of 25 mm (Figure 2.7). Check that the dowelling fits snugly into the hole.

FIGURE 2.6

FIGURE 2.7

12 Mark in the slope at the rear end of the breech, giving a 60° angle to the horizontal, and saw off the waste. Shape the front of the breech with the chisel to round it off and then sandpaper all the surfaces.

13 Mix a quantity of wood glue and assemble all the joints, tapping them fully home with the mallet, and wiping away excess glue. When dry, give another rub down with sandpaper.

14 You can either apply a coat of clear varnish to the wood, or paint it a dark metallic grey.

questions

(a) List the differences between the two types of mortise and tenon joint used in this project. Which do you think is the more difficult to make, and why?

(b) Is the bridle joint in any way similar to the mortise and tenon? If so, what are the similarities? If not, what are the differences?

(c) In Paragraph 10, why are you told to work the spokeshave from both directions towards the centre of the curve?

(d) Drilling a hole into the end-grain of wood (Paragraph 11) is usually harder than drilling across the grain, as in the example of the ship (Project 1). Why do you think this is so? Does it have anything to do with the type of wood you are using? In general, which do you think is easier for drilling into end-grain — softwood or hardwood? For what reason?

exercises

(i) Prepare fully exploded drawings of all the joints used in the gun.

(ii) Think how you could alter the shape and size of the gun, without changing the four types of joint used in it.

(iii) Design a toy or model of your own choice, using exactly the same joints.

project 3
the egg-rack

The egg-rack is a two-tier stand suitable for storing a dozen eggs. It is perfectly stable, and will not easily be knocked over.

how it is designed

The material used for the egg-rack is 13 mm birch-faced plywood, which is strong and comparatively light in weight.

The two racks are attached to the side panels with housing joints, making for a robust and durable structure. The egg holes are spaced at regular intervals along both the racks, and drilled right through the plywood. The two side panels are rounded at the top to make for a simple and plain appearance.

FIGURE 3.1

tool list

Pencil
ruler
square
compasses
tenon saw
coping saw
13 mm bevel chisel
mallet
handbrace with 32 mm centre bit
plane

cutting list

Item	Long mm	Wide mm	Thick mm
2 side panels	230	150	13
2 racks	236	150	13

Note: The grain of the ply surfaces runs along the length of each piece.

how to make it

1 Cut and plane all the pieces to size.

2 Taking the two side panels (Figure 3.2), mark in the semi-circular tops with the compasses set to a radius of 75 mm. Remove the waste with the coping saw (Figure 3.3), working the blade 2 mm or so on the waste side of the line, and finish off the work with sandpaper.

3 Measure and mark the housing joint grooves on the inner faces of the sides with the pencil and square. The width of the groove should be equal to the 13 mm thickness of the plywood.

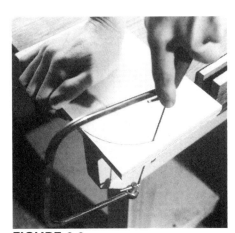

FIGURE 3.3

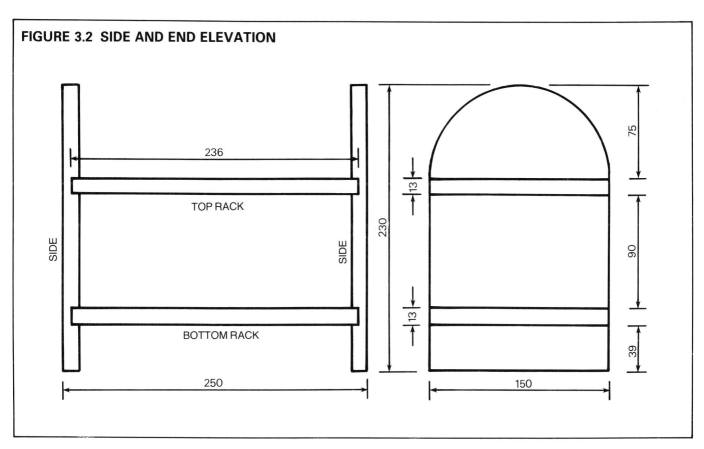

FIGURE 3.2 SIDE AND END ELEVATION

236

TOP RACK

SIDE SIDE

BOTTOM RACK

230

250

75

13

90

13

39

150

4   Saw on the waste side of these lines with the tenon saw, cutting to a depth of 6 mm. Remove the waste from the grooves with the 13 mm chisel, holding the panel against the bench-stop (Figure 3.4).

FIGURE 3.4

5   When all four grooves have been cut, check the fitting of the joints by tapping the racks into position. If all is well, dismantle the joints.

6   Measure and mark the centres of the egg-holes, six in each rack (Figure 3.5). Drill out the holes with the

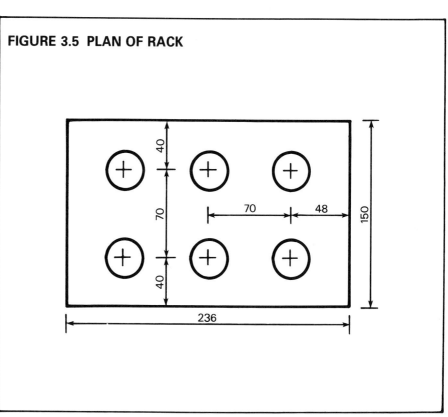

FIGURE 3.5 PLAN OF RACK

40

70

40

70

48

150

236

FIGURE 3.6

handbrace and the 32 mm centre bit, holding the rack firmly against the bench-stop to prevent it from rotating with the motion of the drill (Figure 3.6). Do not attempt to bore straight through, but check to see when the tip of the drill breaks through on the other side of the rack.

7 Turn the rack over and continue drilling from that side, so that the drill-holes meet halfway through, at which point the waste can be removed. Repeat the same procedure for the other eleven holes, and finally rub down the inside edges with fine sandpaper.

8 Mix a quantity of wood glue and apply it with a small brush to the grooves. Assemble all the joints, tapping them fully home, and wipe away excess glue with a moist rag. Place the completed egg-rack to one side for the glue to harden.

9 Give the egg-rack another rub down with fine sandpaper, and finally apply two coats of clear varnish.

questions

(a) Why do you think plywood is the best material to use for this project?

(b) In measuring out the grooves for the housing joints (Paragraph 3), there is no need to make a special point of marking in the depth. Why do you think this is so?

(c) When drilling out the egg-holes with the handbrace and 32 mm centre bit (Paragraph 6), why are you advised not to drill straight through the piece?

exercises

(i) Prepare an exploded three-dimensional drawing of the egg-rack.

(ii) Eggs are graded in a variety of sizes — our design is suitable for the medium size. Redesign and alter the scale of the whole egg-rack, including the diameter of the egg-holes, for the smallest and largest size of egg that you can buy in the shops — including chocolate eggs.

(iii) One way of creating a more original design of your own is to cut away sections in the side panels, such as removing portions from the base to produce two feet. This type of work is best done with card templates. Use your imagination to make different designs.

project 4
the teapot stand

The teapot stand is a useful item for the household, keeping heat from the pot, or indeed a coffee percolator, away from the table surface.

how it is designed

The main part of the stand, in other words the flat surface upon which hot objects are placed, is a quarry tile measuring 152 mm square and 9 mm thick. Quarry tiles can be purchased singly quite cheaply, and come in a variety of colours.

The design of the stand splits the square of the tile up into an octagon, or an eight-sided figure, by fitting triangular pieces of wood to each corner and then joining these up with thin matching strips (Figure 4.2).

The joint for the corner pieces is a triangular mortise, cut to match the shape of the tile, and the joining strips are butt-jointed in position. The four triangular mortises are shown as the shaded areas (Figure 4.2).

Any kind of left-over hardwood may be used, depending on what is available in the classroom store, such as oak, chestnut or elm. Our example uses afrormosia.

FIGURE 4.1

tool list

Pencil	hacksaw
ruler	9 mm bevel chisel
square	mallet
mortise gauge	plane
tenon saw	trimming knife

cutting list

Item	Long mm	Wide mm	Thick mm
4 corner blocks	52	52	19
4 joining strips	62	10	19

6 mm-thick cork tile for the 4 triangular pads

how to make it

1 Measure and mark the four triangular corner pieces onto blocks of wood 19 mm thickness, copying the dimensions shown (Figure 4.3). Note that one block of scrap wood has two triangular patterns marked out as economically as possible (Figure 4.4). Use the square, pencil and ruler to mark identical patterns on both the upper and lower faces of the blocks.

FIGURE 4.4

2 Set the pointers of the mortise gauge to the thickness of the tile, which should be 9 mm. Then adjust the fence of the gauge until the pointers mark the 19 mm-thick edge of the wood centrally. Scribe parallel lines along the edge from which the waste is to be removed, making sure that you only mark these lines over the measured distance of 60 mm.

3 Placing the block in the vice, chop out the waste with the 9 mm chisel (Figure 4.5). The procedure is similar to cutting a mortise, except that in this case the mortise is triangular. Start chopping from the centre, working outwards. Follow the triangular shape of the mortise carefully, checking often by slipping the piece over the corner of the tile.

FIGURE 4.5

FIGURE 4.2 PLAN

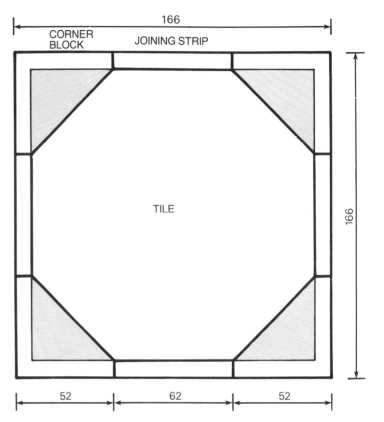

CORNER BLOCK

JOINING STRIP

166

166

TILE

52   62   52

FIGURE 4.3
CORNER BLOCK DIMENSIONS

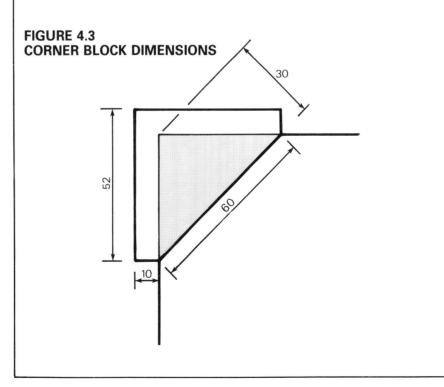

30

52

60

10

4   When all four mortises have been cut, saw the corner pieces roughly to size with the tenon saw, leaving 2 mm of waste beyond the pencil lines.

5   Place the corner pieces in the vice one at a time and plane the edges down to the pencil lines with the smoothing plane.

6   Slide the corner pieces on to the tile and measure the four equal gaps separating them: these gaps should be 62 mm in length. Cut four joining strips from more of the waste wood, each strip measuring 62 mm in length, 10 mm in width and 19 mm in thickness. A light hacksaw and plane are the best tools for this job.

7   Check that all eight pieces fit well around the tile (Figure 4.6).

8   The eight pieces of wood are now ready to be stuck to the tile. It is best

FIGURE 4.6

to use an epoxy resin adhesive, the sort that is supplied with the adhesive in one small tube and the hardener in a second tube.

9   Following the maker's instructions, mix the adhesive

thoroughly and apply it with a flexible plastic spatula. Work it well into each mortise and press the four corner pieces fully home. Finally, apply the glue mixture to the joining strips and fix these in position.

10   When the adhesive has hardened completely after a day or so, lightly sandpaper the surfaces of the wood to remove all traces of surplus adhesive and pencil marks.

11   Cut small triangular pads from a 6 mm-thick cork tile, and stick one pad to the underside of each of the four corners, using a further mixing of adhesive. Leave this to harden.

12   The tile and its wooden surround should be given a coating of semi-matt heat-resisting varnish, which will bring out the grain of the wood and give it an attractive finish.

questions

(a)   Do you think a softwood could be used just as well as a hardwood for this project? If so, why is hardwood recommended?

(b)   When chopping out the four triangular mortises (Paragraph 3), what is the best way of ensuring accuracy in order to avoid cutting out too much or too little waste?

(c)   Paragraph 5 tells you to plane the waste off the corner pieces, with each piece held firmly in the vice. What precautions would you expect to take when planing wood in this way, and why?

(d)   Epoxy resin adhesive is not one of the most commonly used adhesives in woodwork. Why is it used in this particular case?

exercises

(i)   Suppose that you want to make two tea-pot stands of a different size from the one in the example: one of your tiles measures 100 mm square, and the other is 225 mm square. Prepare two separate plans and determine in each case the dimensions of the four corner pieces and the four joining strips.

(ii)   Instead of making a stand with an octagonal, or eight-sided, pattern, adapt the design to create a circular pattern, using four pieces of wood. What additional tool would you have to use in order to make the curved sections?

project 5
the kitchen-roll holder

The kitchen-roll holder is an essential item in most households, making a convenient dispenser for kitchen paper. It has an easily removable spindle which allows the roll to be changed quickly and simply.

FIGURE 5.1

how it is designed

The holder is designed on the principle that a standard kitchen-roll measures 234 mm in width and 120 mm in diameter when full.

As kitchen paper is light in weight, the holder does not need to possess great strength, and it can therefore be assembled with butt joints.

The spindle is a length of dowelling, and this drops into two U-shaped slots cut in the sides. The position of the slots is important: they must hold the spindle far enough from the back and the base panels so that the full roll can revolve without binding.

Any kind of softwood or hardwood may be used, but preferably one that has an attractive grain. For example, you could use pine or Brazilian mahogany.

tool list

Pencil	hacksaw	handbrace with 32 mm centre bit
ruler	6 mm bevel chisel	and no. 8 wood drill
square	mallet	plane
tenon saw		hammer

cutting list

Item	Long mm	Wide mm	Thick mm
2 side members	95	89	19
1 back panel	280	95	9
1 base panel	280	78	9

Item	Long mm	Diameter mm	
1 spindle	258	32	

Note: The grain runs along the length of each piece.

FIGURE 5.2 FRONT ELEVATION

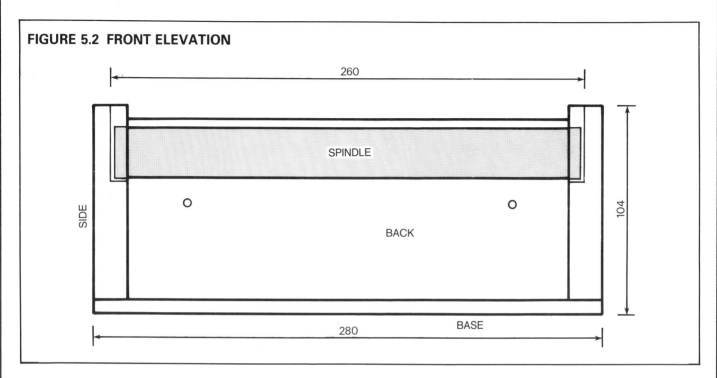

260

SPINDLE

SIDE

104

BACK

280   BASE

how to make it

1 Cut the two side members to size, sawing and planing both pieces into rectangles measuring 95 mm by 89 mm each.

2 Taking the two sides in turn, measure and mark the U-shaped slot at the top of the inside face of each one, referring to the measurements (Figure 5.3). Having determined the position of the slot's centre of curvature, mark this point and drill into it with the 32 mm centre bit mounted in the handbrace, drilling the hole 9 mm into the wood (Figure 5.4).

FIGURE 5.3 SIDE ELEVATION

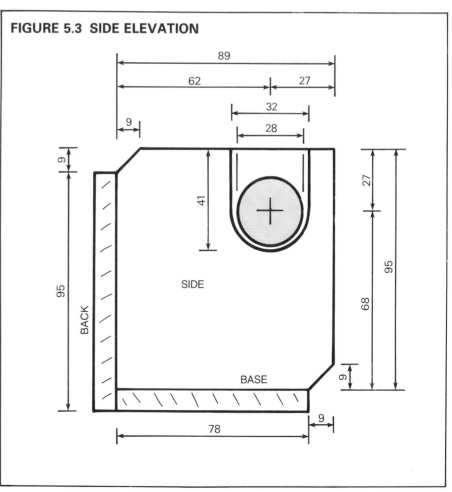

89

62   27

32

9   28

9

41   27

95   95

BACK   SIDE   68

BASE   9

78   9

FIGURE 5.4

FIGURE 5.5

3 Clean out all the waste wood, then chisel out the remainder of the slot, working the 6mm chisel with care to ensure clean edges (Figure 5.5). Repeat the same process for the second slot in its corresponding position on the second side member.

4 Measure out the back and base panels, sawing and planing them to size.

5 Measure and mark the triangular cut away portions at the top and bottom edges of the side members where they meet the upper edge of the back panel and the forward edge of the base panel, trimming off the waste with angled chisel cuts.

6 Drill two holes in the back panel to take no. 8 wall-mounting screws, set in about 50mm from either side.

7 Assemble the four parts of the holder. Mix a quantity of wood glue and apply it to the bottom edges of both side members, placing them in position on the base. Tap small veneer pins through to secure the joint, and repeat the same procedure for the back panel.

8 When the glue has dried and set hard, rub down the assembly with sandpaper to remove pencil marks and traces of glue. Round off the sharp edges and corners.

9 Apply two coats of polyurethane varnish, either matt or gloss. While this is drying, cut the spindle from a length of 32mm diameter dowelling. Stain it a light brown colour and finish off with varnish.

questions

(a) What must you be careful to guard against when drilling the 9mm-deep hole for the U-shaped slot in Paragraph 2?

(b) Before chiselling out the remainder of the slot (Paragraph 3), what precaution should you take in order to prevent the chisel from removing good wood?

(c) Why are the veneer pins used to support the butt joints?

(d) What is the best way of applying stain or varnish smoothly and evenly all around the spindle without getting them on your fingers, and subsequently allowing them to dry?

exercises

(i) Adapt the design of the kitchen-roll holder to create a spice rack, or a rack to hold small jam-jars. You will obviously need to think about adding and removing certain parts. Remember also that glass jars weigh more than kitchen paper — so is the butt joint going to be strong enough to hold the rack together? Use alternative joints in your design.

(ii) Working to a larger or smaller scale, think of other uses for the kitchen-roll holder design. For example, it could be reduced in size and used to hold toilet paper. Work out the appropriate dimensions for yourself.

project 6
the dog box

The dog box is a home for the family pet. It is a collapsible six-sided box that comes apart easily for cleaning, and folds up so that it can be stored away in the back of the car when travelling on holiday.

how it is designed

The box is designed to have a regular hexagonal or six-sided base with the floor mounted one-third of the way up, and a five-sided upper row with one side left open for access (Figures 6.2 and 6.3).

All the side panels are hinged together, and as each piece is cut from tongued-and-grooved wood, the upper row simply slots onto the base. The floor panels likewise slot into each other, and are attached to the base with dowelled pegs. One of the hinges in the base — it does not matter which one — has a removable hinge-pin so that the six sides can be opened up and detached from the floor.

The illustrated example is a reasonable size for a small dog, but you will have to vary the dimensions to suit an average-sized or a much larger dog, or indeed a very small cat.

The wood used is tongued-and-grooved red deal. You could start with plain boards and cut your own tongues and grooves using a plough plane. An alternative wood is Parana pine.

FIGURE 6.1

tool list

Pencil	tenon saw	mallet	plane
ruler	hacksaw	handbrace with	bradawl
square	25 mm bevel chisel	6 mm centre bit	screwdriver

cutting list

Item	Long mm	Wide mm	Thick mm
11 sides	290	150	19
2 long floorboards	580	150	19
2 short floorboards	420	150	19
	Long mm	Diameter mm	
6 dowelled pegs	25	6	

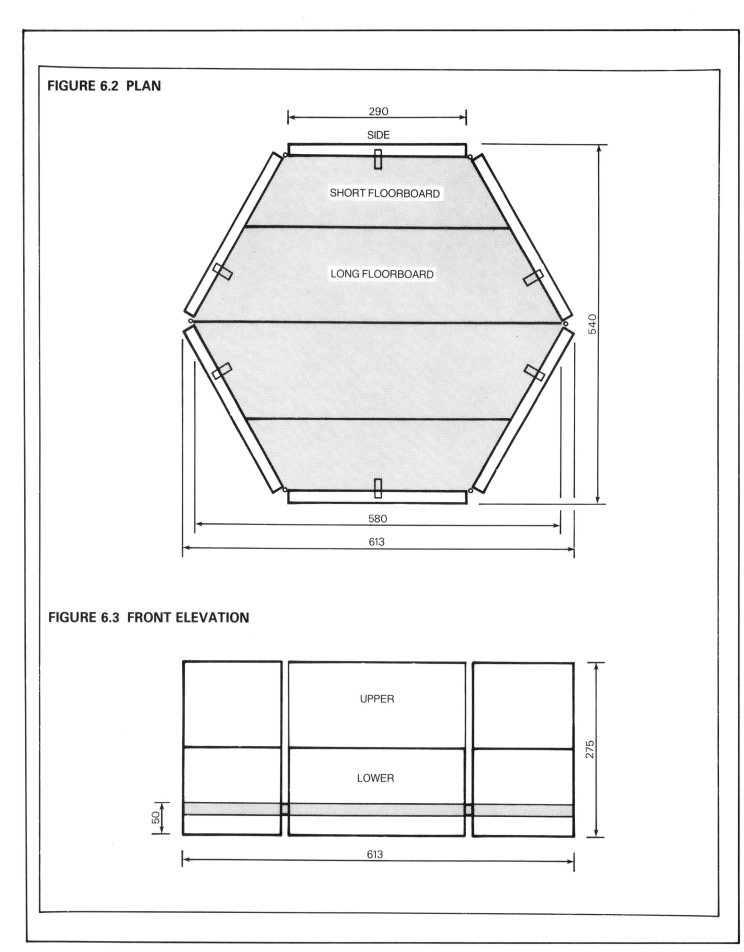

FIGURE 6.2 PLAN

290

SIDE

SHORT FLOORBOARD

LONG FLOORBOARD

540

580

613

FIGURE 6.3 FRONT ELEVATION

UPPER

LOWER

275

50

613

how to make it

1 Measure and cut all eleven side pieces to length and plane the ends square. Check that they are all identical.

FIGURE 6.4

2 Take six of the eleven pieces, five from the entire upper row and one from the base, and plane off the tongues (Figure 6.4). Chamfer the edges where the joints meet between the upper and lower levels, to give a V-shape (Figure 6.5).

3 All six sides of the base now have to be hinged together, requiring six hinges to close the hexagon completely. A further four hinges are needed for the five sides of the upper row. The ten hinges may be cut from a single long piano hinge, which is obtainable from most ironmongers. Using the hacksaw, cut the piano hinge up into ten lengths of 120 mm each, arranging if possible for the screw holes to be regularly spaced out.

4 Taking each hinge and side piece in turn, place the hinge at the edge of the wood, 10 mm up from the bottom, and mark around it with a pencil (Figure 6.6). Score around this line with the 25 mm chisel, tapping it with the mallet to make an impression, then work the chisel carefully to cut a 1 mm-deep recess into which the hinge will fit.

5 When the recess is complete, position the hinge and mark in the screw holes with the bradawl. The

FIGURE 6.6

hinge is then fixed in place with small brass screws.

6 Line up the neighbouring side piece and measure around the hinge's second flap, ensuring that the sides are exactly level. Continue joining up the sides until all six lengths of the base are hinged in a straight line with five hinges, leaving one hinge remaining to link up the two extreme ends.

7 The final hinge is deliberately split apart, enabling the base to be put together and dismantled whenever it is desired. Use a thin rod to punch out the hinge-pin from the knuckle, so that the two halves of the hinge can be separated. Then bend the pin 10 mm from one end in the form of an L: this will allow the pin to be inserted into or extracted from the hinge at will.

8 Measure and cut out the recesses for the split hinge in the usual way, and assemble the five sides of the upper row in the same manner.

9 Join up the base and arrange the sides so that they form a regular hexagon. By measuring the distance between all opposite sides and making slight adjustments to their position where necessary, a regular shape will be achieved.

10 Slot the four floor panels together, with the two longer panels in the middle, and place the base on top of these, copying the pattern shown in Figure 6.2. Mark around the inside bottom edge of the base, pencilling a line around the four floor panels.

FIGURE 6.5

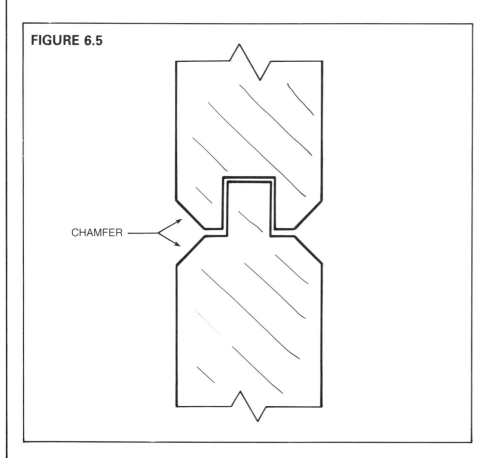

CHAMFER

11 Saw and plane each of the floor panels to size. When the floorboards slot together satisfactorily within the base, cut away small notches at each corner to fit around the hinge knuckles.

12 Unfold the six sides of the base, laying them out flat, and measure in the position of the floor panels, which are mounted 50 mm up from the bottom. Each panel is held in position by means of dowel pegs. These pegs are glued into the panels, and their projecting ends fit into holes cut in the inside faces of the base. It does not matter exactly where these pegs and holes go, except that they must line up precisely with one another.

13 Mark the positions of the pegs with the pencil and square (Figure

FIGURE 6.7

6.7) and drill out the holes with the handbrace and the 6 mm centre bit. Glue the pegs into the holes in the floor panels with wood glue (Figure 6.8).

14 When the glue has set hard, sandpaper all the surfaces. You can

FIGURE 6.8

either leave the wood in its natural colour, or apply one of a wide variety of wood stains, finishing with a coat of glaze. Finally assemble the floorboards inside the base, fit the hinge-pin and drop the upper row into place.

questions

(a) What precaution must you take when planing the ends of all the side pieces square (Paragraph 1)?

(b) The shape of the box is described as a regular hexagon. What does the word 'regular' mean?

exercises

(i) Work out on paper how much material would be needed to make a six-sided box where each side measures 145 mm or half the length of the illustrated example; and secondly for a box where the side measures 435 mm, or one and a half times the example. Assume that you use tongued-and-grooved wood of the same size throughout, 150 mm in width and 19 mm thick.

(ii) Think up your own ideas for using this type of box for other purposes than housing the family dog or cat. For example, if you attached the base with floorboards to the wall, it would make a good dartboard surround.

project 7
the box calendar

This type of calendar is very useful because the date number that appears in the big window can be altered together with the day and the month seen in the two smaller windows to give you any date you want. It is a permanent calendar, and can be used every year.

how it is designed

The calendar is made in three main sections: a solid base, a hollow box and solid top. The front and side elevations are shown in Figures 7.2 and 7.3 respectively, the plan in Figure 7.6.

The box has four rollers inside it to carry all the information, with finger-knobs projecting at both sides to turn the rollers around. Two of the rollers are large in diameter and the other two are small. All four rollers are reduced to a lesser diameter at their ends to pass through the holes drilled in the sides of the box.

The joints used in the calendar's construction are the housing joint, fitting the front and back panels of the box to the sides, and butt joints attaching the finished box to the base and the top.

The wood in the illustrated example is afrormosia, which is a hardwood, but other woods like pine or deal, which are both softwoods, can be used equally well. Alternative hardwoods are iroko, oak or Brazilian mahogany.

tool list

Pencil
ruler
square
mortise gauge
tenon saw
6 mm bevel chisel
19 mm bevel chisel
mallet
handbrace with 9 mm twist drill
    and 13 mm centre bit
plane
plough plane with 9 mm cutter
lathe

FIGURE 7.1

cutting list

Item	Long mm	Wide mm	Thick mm
1 front panel	130	98	9
1 back panel	130	98	9
2 side panels	130	70	9
1 base	152	112	19
1 top	120	80	19

	Long mm	Diameter mm	
2 large rollers	140	28	
2 small rollers	140	16	

A small quantity of thin scrap plywood

Note: The grain runs along the length of each piece.

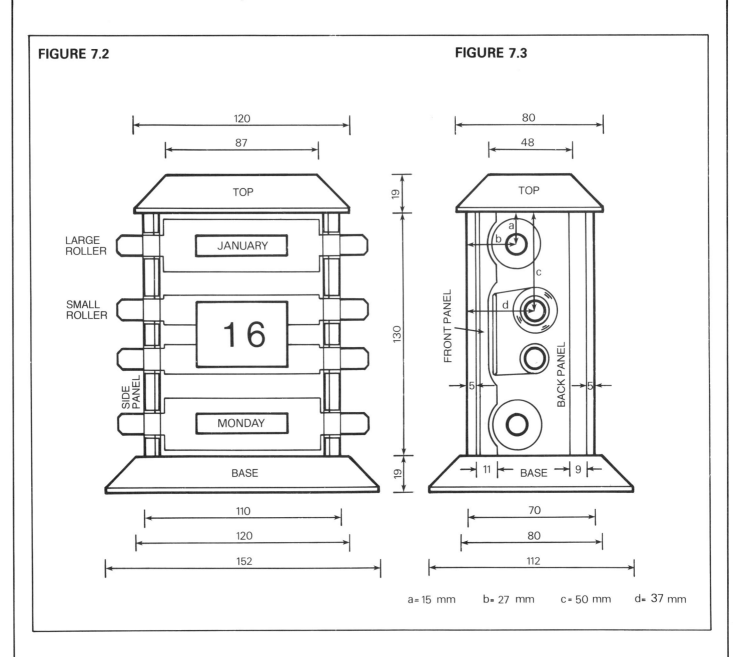

FIGURE 7.2

120
87

TOP

LARGE
ROLLER — JANUARY

SMALL
ROLLER — 16

SIDE
PANEL

MONDAY

BASE

19
130
19

110
120
152

FIGURE 7.3

80
48

TOP

FRONT PANEL

a
b

c

d

BACK PANEL

5   5

11   BASE   9

70
80
112

a = 15 mm   b = 27 mm   c = 50 mm   d = 37 mm

how to make it

1 Start by making the base and top. These are very similar in the way they are both cut and chamfered, differing only in size. For the base, cut a 152 mm by 112 mm rectangle of wood from 19 mm-thick material.

2 Set the mortise gauge (or marking gauge) to 17 mm and score a single line around all four edges of the piece. The 2 mm left-over portion gives a narrow decorative facing at the bottom.

3 Mark a rectangle measuring 120 mm by 80 mm centrally on the upper surface in pencil, then place the wood lengthways in the vice and work the plane at an angle in the direction of the grain, chamfering between the marked-out lines (Figure 7.4). Repeat for the opposite edge until two chamfers are complete.

4 Because it is harder to plane wood successfully across the grain, an alternative method is used for the remaining two chamfers. Clamp the piece firmly to the bench, or hold it

FIGURE 7.4

FIGURE 7.5

securely against the bench-stop, and chisel off the waste, removing a little at a time, to achieve the same chamfer effect (Figure 7.5). Use the widest chisel you can, and make sure it is perfectly sharp before starting.

5 Sandpaper the base and set it aside.

6 Repeat the same process for the top piece, this time cutting a 120 mm by 80 mm rectangle of wood from the same 19 mm-thick material. Mark a rectangle of 87 mm by 48 mm on its uppermost surface, and use the same 17 mm setting for the marker gauge to score around the edges.

7 Having completed the base and top sections, you are now ready to make the box. This is constructed by making use of the housing joint (Figures 7.6 and 7.7). Measure out the front, back and side pieces, squaring each one accurately, cutting up and planing to the correct length and width.

8 The housing joint consists of grooves cut in the sides to house the edges of both the front and back panels. When marking out these grooves, note that whereas the back groove is 9 mm wide to match exactly the thickness of the wood, an extra 2 mm is added to the front groove for a piece of glass to slide in, giving a groove width of 11 mm.

9 Use the plough plane fitted with a 9 mm cutter to make the grooves. The fence of the plane should be adjusted so that it cuts 5 mm in from the edge,

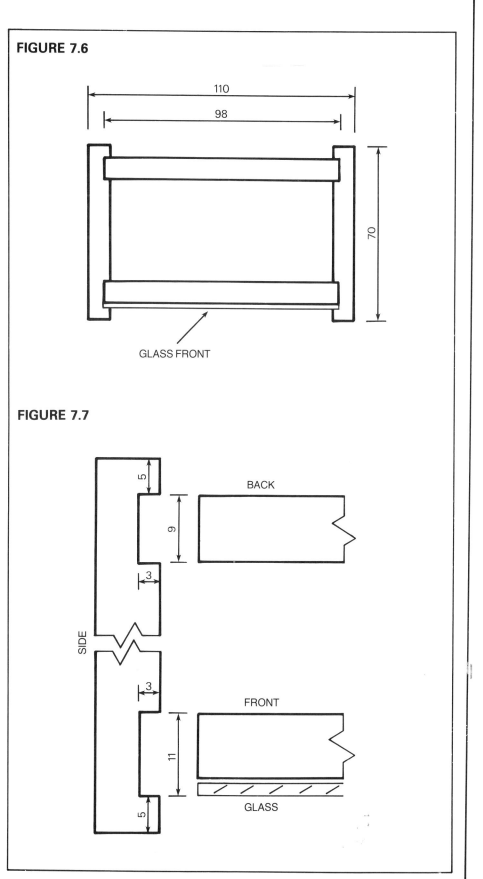

FIGURE 7.6

110

98

70

GLASS FRONT

FIGURE 7.7

SIDE

5

9

3

3

11

5

BACK

FRONT

GLASS

FIGURE 7.8

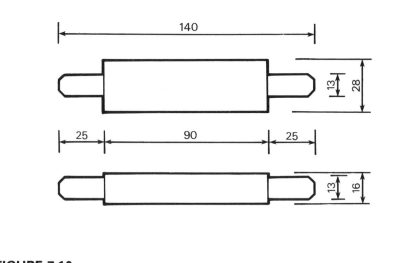

FIGURE 7.9

FIGURE 7.10

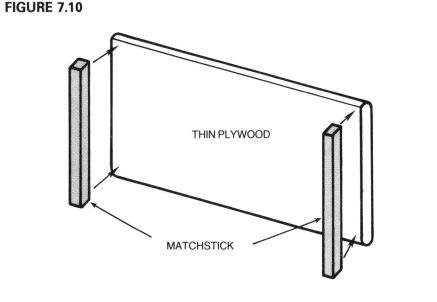

THIN PLYWOOD

MATCHSTICK

and the depth gauge set to give a depth of 3 mm (Figure 7.8).

10 For the 11 mm housing groove, keep the same 9 mm cutter in the plough plane but move the fence outwards by 2 mm to increase the width of the groove by the required amount. The depth, of course, remains the same.

11 Both of the side pieces now have four 13 mm diameter holes drilled in them for the rollers to pass through. Mark the holes in the positions shown (Figure 7.3), and drill out with the 13 mm diameter centre bit mounted in the handbrace. Drill the wood in two stages: firstly by boring halfway through from one side until the point of the bit just emerges, and then turning the wood over to complete the hole from the other side.

12 Mark out the three windows in the front panel, drawing the rectangular boxes clearly on the surface of the wood in pencil. Most of the waste can be removed quickly by drilling a series of holes within each box, but remember the precaution mentioned in the previous paragraph and do not drill right through in one go.

13 Chop out the remainder of the waste using the chisel and mallet, working a clean straight edge on all four sides of each window. Then determine which is to be the outside face of the front panel, and mark on its inner face the three curved

channels into which the two big rollers and the numeral band will fit.

14 Having marked the channels, remove the waste by sawing a series of lines along their length and pare off the unwanted wood with the 6 mm chisel. Smooth the curved surfaces by wrapping a piece of sandpaper around a length of 28 mm diameter dowelling and rubbing this along the channels.

15 Cut the two large rollers from 28 mm diameter dowelling to a length of 140 mm, and the two small rollers

likewise from 16 mm diameter dowelling (Figure 7.9). All the rollers have 25 mm at each end reduced to a diameter of 13 mm, leaving 90 mm of full diameter roller to rest inside the calendar. The best way of running down the ends is to use the lathe.

16 Temporarily assemble the box with the rollers in position to check that they fit well and can be turned easily without binding.

17 Next, make the wooden backrest to fit behind the large numeral window (Figure 7.10). Cut this from thin scrap plywood measuring 80 mm by 35 mm, round off the top and bottom edges with fine sandpaper and glue matchstick spacers in position as shown. Then glue the backrest in place in the channel behind the numeral window.

18 Treat all the outside surfaces of the calendar box, the top and the base with teak oil, finishing with a polish. An alternative is to use polyurethane varnish, preferably the semi-matt variety. Do not oil or varnish the parts that will receive glue when the various pieces are stuck together.

19 Before finally assembling the box, print the lettering for the day

and the month on strips of plain white paper using small dry-print lettering available from stationery shops, and then stick the paper to the rollers.

20 The numeral band is 70 mm-width white ribbon, obtainable from fabric shops and a length of 1 metre is required. Numbers from 1 to 31 are stencilled onto the ribbon with a plastic lettering stencil, and the outlines filled in with black embroidery pen or any other black ball-point pen. Perhaps you could persuade your art teacher to give you some help with this.

21 Thread the numeral band through its backrest and glue both

ends to their respective rollers with adhesive. Place the other two rollers in position and glue the box together at each of its housing joints.

22 The box is butt-jointed to the base and the top, relying on the strength of the glue to hold the assembly together. Glue the box to the base, slide a piece of picture glass measuring 130 mm by 98 mm and 2 mm thick into its slot in the front panel, and glue the top down.

23 Finally stick a piece of green felt to the underside of the base with adhesive to soften its contact with the desk or table top.

questions

(a) If you had either hard or softwood available for this project, which of the two would you choose, and why?

(b) Paragraph 4 says that it is harder to plane wood successfully across the grain. Why do you think this is so, and what precautions must you take if you attempt this method?

(c) Paragraphs 11 and 12 tell you to drill right through a piece of wood in two stages: firstly by boring halfway through from one side and then turning the wood over to complete the hole from the other side. Why? Can you think of a method that would allow you to drill straight through in one go?

(d) In Paragraphs 13 and 14 you are told to mark and cut out three curved channels into which the two big rollers and the numeral band fit. What is the purpose of these channels, and why must they not be cut too deep?

(e) The rollers are best turned on the lathe (Paragraph 15). Can you think of an alternative method, using handtools? Describe how you would set about doing it.

(f) Why is the wooden backrest (Paragraph 17) an important part of the calendar?

(g) The calendar box is butt-jointed to the base and the top (Paragraph 22). Why is this type of joint, a very simple one, suitable here in particular?

exercises

(i) Prepare a fully exploded three-dimensional drawing of the housing joint.

(ii) Glass is not the only material suitable for fitting into the front panel groove — other clear materials can be used. Suggest possible alternatives, and state why these might mean amending the design slightly.

(iii) The basic idea of the box calendar can be adapted to different dimensions, perhaps even to be mounted on a wall. How could our example be altered for this purpose, and what are the main points that you would have to watch out for?

(iv) Taking Exercise (iii) a stage further, consider the design of the box calendar but remove the four rollers and the date information to leave simply the box, the base and the top. With a possible alteration in scale, think of other uses for the basic design and show clearly how you would adapt and modify it.

project 8
the picnic table

This type of picnic table is ideal for several reasons. It is of a low, sturdy construction and will not be easily put off-balance. The legs fold up compactly into the table so that it will not take up much room in the car. It can also be used as a spare table in the lounge at home, particularly if it is well polished.

how it is designed

As this table is designed mainly to serve an outdoor picnic, whether in the heart of the country, by the seaside or in the lay-by of some fast main road, it has to fulfil certain requirements.

It must be large enough to accommodate the plates and cutlery of up to four people, but it must also store away easily in the back of the car. The legs must be low to give stability in a strong wind, and the top surface slatted so that spilt drinks can run away harmlessly.

Most of the joints are mortise and tenons, the remainder being halved joints. The leg assemblies are hinged to the table top with galvanised bolts and wing-nuts.

For this sort of table it is preferable to use hardwood. Our example is made from iroko, which is a very strong and durable hardwood though it does have some dulling effect on the sharp edge of the chisel, which is an obvious penalty. Suggested alternatives are agba or utile.

FIGURE 8.1

tool list

Pencil	hacksaw	countersink
ruler	6 mm bevel chisel	plane
square	mallet	screwdriver
mortise gauge	handbrace with 4 mm and 2 mm	
tenon saw	twist drills	

cutting list

Item	Long mm	Wide mm	Thick mm
2 side members	800	32	16
2 crosspieces	468 (492)	32	16
6 slats	718 (734)	48	16
4 legs	355	32	16
2 crossbars	465	32	16

Note: The figures in brackets above are for total length including tenons.

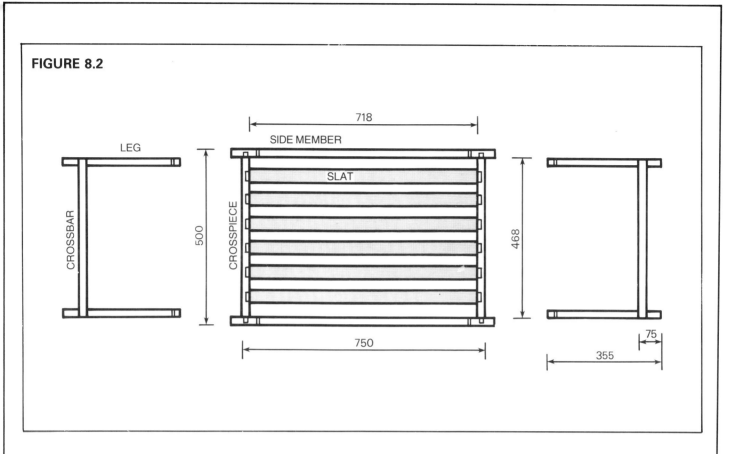

FIGURE 8.2

LEG

CROSSBAR

SIDE MEMBER

SLAT

CROSSPIECE

718

500

468

750

355

75

how to make it

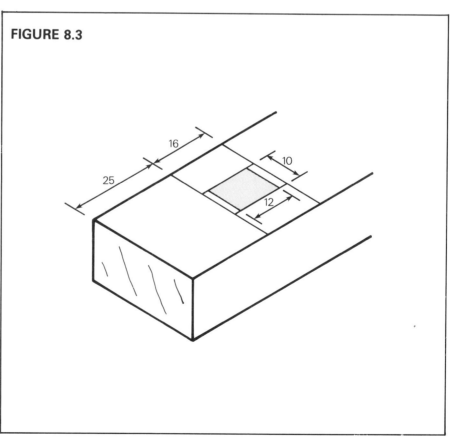

FIGURE 8.3

25

16

10

12

1 Measure and cut the two side members to length. Mark off 25 mm at each end for the projections of the side members beyond the crosspieces (Figure 8.2).

2 Mark in the positions of the mortises (Figure 8.3), allowing for the 25 mm projections. With the square, pencil and ruler, measure and mark in the lines that show the total width of the crosspiece, 16 mm. Set the mortise gauge to one-third the width of the side member, which is approximately 10 mm. Adjust the fence of the gauge so that the two pointers scribe the wood centrally, and score two parallel marks between the pencil lines. Set in the mortise by 2 mm from each of these lines, giving it a length of 12 mm.

3 Clamp the piece securely in the vice, and chop out the waste wood using the 6 mm chisel. Start in the middle of the marked-out area and work outwards in the direction of the

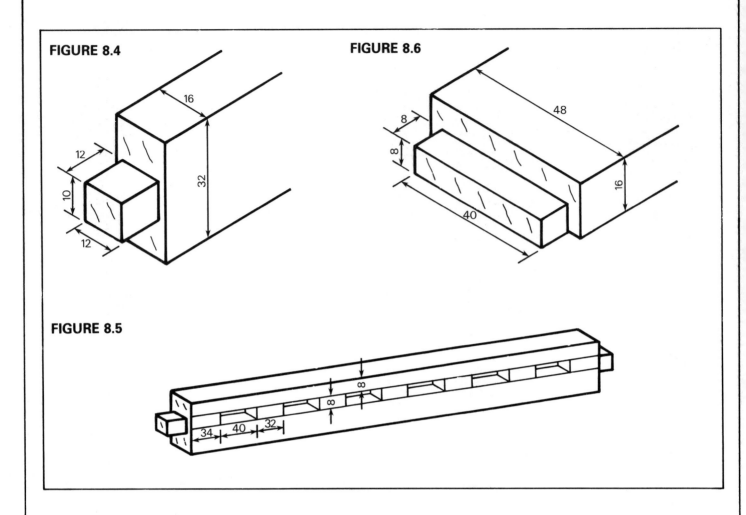

FIGURE 8.4

16

12

10

12

32

FIGURE 8.6

8

8

48

16

40

FIGURE 8.5

8

8

34 40 32

grain. Check the depth of the mortise regularly as you are cutting it, until it reaches a depth of 12 mm, or three-quarters the thickness of the wood.

4 When both side members have had their mortises cut, measure for the tenons at either end of the crosspieces. Each tenon is 12 mm in length, in order to match exactly the depth of the mortise. Measure out this amount and square a line right around the wood.

5 Using the mortise gauge with its pointers and fence still set as before, score two parallel marks on both the 32 mm-width faces and join these up by marking the end of the wood.

6 Cut the tenon, following the standard procedure. When the two shoulders have been removed, mark in the two remaining shoulders which are both 2 mm thick and cut these

away using the hacksaw to leave the four-shouldered tenon (Figure 8.4).

7 File the tenon to a smooth finish and fit it into the mortise, tapping it gently home with the mallet. If you feel any resistance, do not force it or the wood may split. Instead, pare off small slivers of wood from the mortise, and keep filing the tenon, until the joint fits well.

8 The next step is to cut six mortises in each of the two crosspieces to receive the six slats. First, mark the width of each mortise, 40 mm, each one being spaced 32 mm from its neighbour (Figure 8.5). Note, however, that the distance between the end mortises and the edges of the crosspiece is 34 mm.

9 Set the mortise gauge to 8 mm, and adjust the fence of the gauge so that the mortises are placed 8 mm

down from the top of both crosspieces. Mark in all six mortises.

10 Clamp the piece in the vice and chop out the mortises with the 6 mm chisel to a depth of 8 mm.

11 Measure and cut the six slats to an overall length of 734 mm each, then mark in the tenons at both ends. Use the mortise gauge in the same setting. The tenons here are of the barefaced type, where the main shoulder is cut on one side only. This is a top-edged shoulder, which effectively conceals the mortise from view. Mark each tenon to a depth of 8 mm.

12 Cut out in the usual way, then mark in 4 mm side shoulders and remove these too (Figure 8.6). Check that all of the twelve joints fit easily, tapping smoothly into place.

FIGURE 8.7

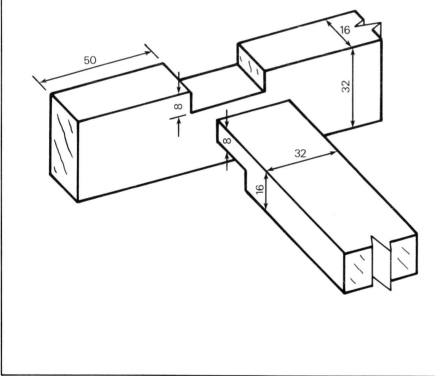

SIDE MEMBER → 6 ←

CROSS-
PIECE

LEG

FIGURE 8.8

50

8

8

16

32

32

16

15 At the same time, drill corresponding holes through the side members. Note from Figure 8.7 that the legs are best angled outwards for stability. After measuring and drilling the hole in the side member, round off the one top corner of the leg, using a two penny piece and pencil to draw in the curve. Lightly plane away the waste.

16 Next, mark out the halved joints used to join the crossbars to the legs. Each joint is placed 50 mm from the bottom end of the leg. The joint is cut 8 mm deep into the leg and 8 mm into the crossbar (Figure 8.8). Measure and mark the lines with pencil, ruler and square.

17 Remove the waste from the leg. Firstly, cut with the tenon saw down to the 8 mm depth line, working on the waste side of the two width lines. Then chisel out the waste from between the two saw cuts, chopping out the unwanted wood a little at a time.

18 The crossbar waste is removed in the same way as cutting a tenon shoulder. When all four halved joints are complete, check that they fit together accurately.

19 The table is now ready for assembly. Mix a quantity of wood glue and apply it with a small brush to each of the twelve mortise and tenon joints between the table slats and the two crosspieces. Tap the joints together with a clean block of scrap wood and the mallet, and then cramp up the work. Wipe away any excess glue with a moist rag.

20 When the glue has set hard, remove the cramps and prepare to fit the side members to the crosspieces. If all the joints have been measured and cut accurately, these should now slide easily into place. As the strength of the table assembly depends on the four remaining mortise and tenon joints, they are secured with screws and glue.

21 The process of screwing together a mortise and tenon is known as draw-boring. A small 2 mm countersunk hole is drilled through

13 The four legs are prepared next. First, cut these to length and then measure and mark the holes for the hinges. Each hole is placed centrally on the 32 mm-width face, set at a distance of 16 mm from the top end.

14 Drill out with the 4 mm twist drill mounted in the handbrace. Clamp the piece tightly onto some waste material in the vice to prevent the drill from splitting the under-surface as it breaks through.

FIGURE 8.9

the mortise (Figure 8.9), and deliberately off-set through the tenon to pull the joint tightly together. The screws are brass, measuring 19 mm in

length and 3 mm in diameter. Mix more glue, apply it to the joints and drive in the screws.

22   Drill holes for the halved joints of the leg assemblies, and glue and screw these together.

23   When dry, thoroughly sandpaper all the surfaces to remove pencil reference marks and traces of glue. If desired, brush on a dark oak stain and when this is dry, coat with teak oil or varnish. If oil is preferred, finish off with wax polish.

24   The leg assemblies can now be slid inside the table framework, and

FIGURE 8.10

hinged (Figure 8.10). The hinges are galvanised 39 mm by 4 mm bolts, plain washers and wing nuts.

questions

(a)   In Paragraph 1, why are the mortises set in by 25 mm from each end of the side members?

(b)   After drilling the hinge-holes in the legs and side members (Paragraph 15), what is the reason for rounding off the one top corner of each leg?

(c)   Strictly speaking, the halved joints used to join the crossbars to the legs (Paragraph 16) are not pure 'halves'. Can you see why?

(d)   Why is the draw-boring method used in Paragraph 21 particularly important in the assembly of the table top?

exercises

(i)   By altering the size and proportions, think of alternative uses for this design, other than simply a picnic table.

(ii)   Redesign the table top, using different sizes of slats and arranging for greater or smaller gaps in between the slats.

(iii)   Work out the cost of making the picnic table using different types of wood, such as the alternatives like agba and utile already mentioned.

project 9
the lighthouse

The model lighthouse is an attractive ornament for the home, and could be used as a desk paperweight. It is primarily intended to give practice in the use of the lathe, and in particular the skill of woodturning.

You should already have a reasonable knowledge of how to use the lathe and be able to manipulate the special woodturning tools before attempting this project.

how it is designed

The lighthouse is made in two separate parts: the main tower of the lighthouse itself, and a flat base.

Two types of woodturning are employed: spindle-turning is used for the lighthouse, and face-plate work for the base.

Apart from the base, the lighthouse is divided into six sections which each require special attention. Taking these in order, the sections are: (A) the short cylindrical foundation; (B) the tapered tower; (C) the walkway or gantry beneath the lamproom; (D) the lamproom; (E) the roof ledge above the lamproom; (F) the conical roof (Figure 9.2).

The base is a solid piece of wood turned to a circle with a simple curve added to imitate the waves of the sea.

The lighthouse is fixed to the base by working a shallow recess into the base, equal in diameter to the foundation (A), and glued in position.

The wood used in the illustrated example is oak for the lighthouse and afrormosia for the base, but other types of hardwood are suitable. Some are obviously better suited to woodturning than others, but oak and afrormosia are good to work with — though you must beware of the dust from afrormosia — and so are ash, beech and sycamore. Alternatively, you could select a softwood, such as pine or yew.

tool list

Pencil
ruler
pair of compasses
handsaw
chisel
plane
screwdriver
spindle gouge
skew chisel
parting tool
lathe

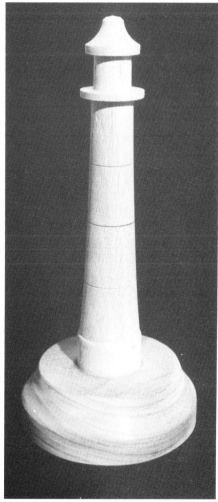

FIGURE 9.1

cutting list

Item	Long mm	Wide mm	Thick mm
1 lighthouse	220	50	50
1 base	125	125	38

Note: Both parts are turned from solid rectangular blocks of wood — often bits of scrap are ideal.

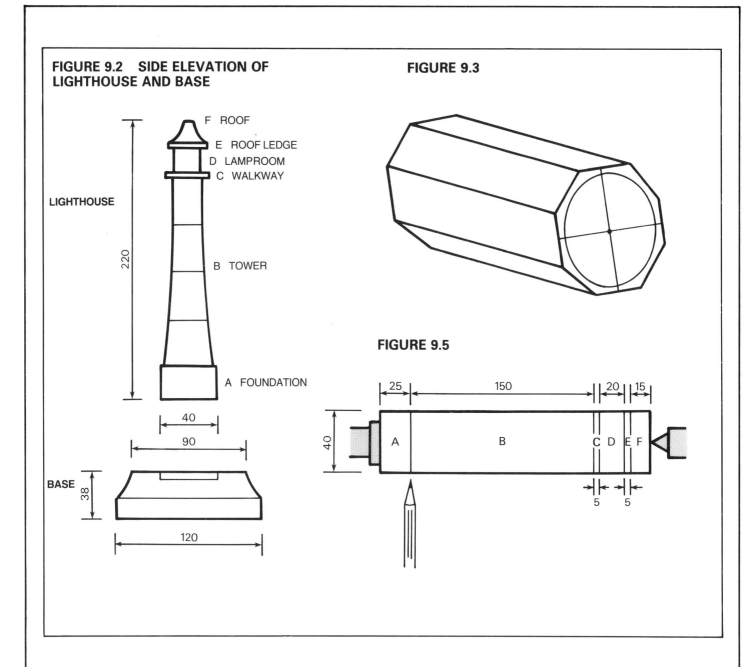

FIGURE 9.2 SIDE ELEVATION OF LIGHTHOUSE AND BASE

F ROOF
E ROOF LEDGE
D LAMPROOM
C WALKWAY

LIGHTHOUSE

220

B TOWER

A FOUNDATION

40

90

BASE

38

120

FIGURE 9.3

FIGURE 9.5

25 · 150 · 20 · 15

40

A B C D E F

5 · 5

how to make it

1 Cut the square-section block of wood for the lighthouse to length. Pencil in diagonal lines to find the centre at both ends and draw a circle with the pair of compasses to a radius of 20 mm. Place the wood in the vice and plane off the edges to make it roughly cylindrical (Figure 9.3).

2 Mount the piece between the headstock and tailstock of the lathe, tightening it up so that there is no lateral movement. Adjust the position

of the tool-rest so that it is slightly below the centre-line of the work and close to it.

3 Wearing protective glasses to safeguard the eyes, start the lathe and use the spindle gouge to rough the work into a perfectly round cylinder of 40 mm diameter (Figure 9.4). The best result is always achieved by using the carving rather than the scraping action.

4 Mark out the divisions between the six different sections by applying the pencil to the spinning cylinder.

There should be five pencil lines (Figure 9.5), marked at the distances indicated.

FIGURE 9.4

5 Form the five divisions with the parting tool, allowing it to work prominent shoulders for the walkway (C) and the roof ledge (E), as shown in Figure 9.6.

FIGURE 9.6

6 Rebate the cylindrical lamproom (D) by careful manipulation of the parting tool, working it in a single steady movement between the two shoulders.

7 Turn the conical roof (F) with the spindle gouge, producing a gentle taper towards the end (Figure 9.7). Do not work it down too deeply yet, otherwise you will weaken its contact with the tailstock and risk unbalancing the work.

FIGURE 9.7

8 Taper and curve the main tower (B) with the spindle gouge, moving it along the tool-rest and applying greatest pressure at the narrowest part of the taper (Figure 9.8). When

FIGURE 9.8

FIGURE 9.9

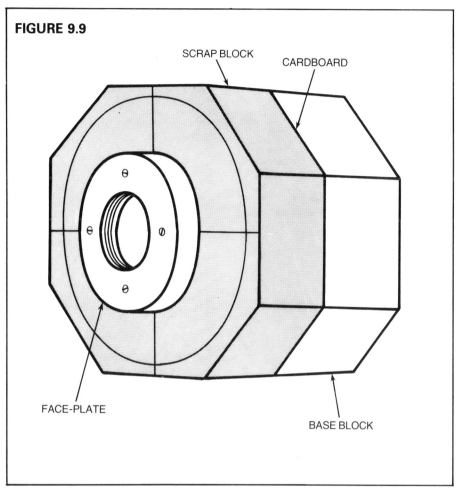

SCRAP BLOCK

CARDBOARD

FACE-PLATE

BASE BLOCK

this is complete, trim the shoulders at the ends of the section with the parting tool.

9 Turn the foundation (A) and work with the spindle gouge to produce a smooth cylindrical finish. Square off the end of the piece with the skew chisel to give a flat base.

10 Sandpaper the lighthouse with a fine-grade paper held firmly on a flexible rubber pad. Finally turn the three decorative grooves on the tower (B) (as in Figure 9.1) with the skew chisel, cutting to a depth of 1 mm or so.

11 Complete the turning of the conical roof with the spindle gouge, then remove the lighthouse from the lathe and trim the top, rubbing down with fine sandpaper.

12 Take the block of wood for the base and glue it to a scrap block of similar size, with a sandwich of cardboard in between. Clamp these tightly together whilst the glue dries and hardens. The purpose of the cardboard is to allow the two pieces of wood to be separated easily after the lathe-work is complete. Mark a circle on its square face with the pair of compasses to a radius of 60 mm, then saw the wood to an octagonal or eight-sided block and screw it centrally onto the face-plate (Figure 9.9). Attach the face-plate to the lathe.

13 Turn the base and rough out the work with the spindle gouge, producing a round block. Continue working the gouge to make the curve.

14 Cut a recess in the centre of the block, equal in diameter to the

FIGURE 9.10

lighthouse foundation (A), using the parting tool (Figure 9.10). The recess should be at least 4 mm deep. Sandpaper the base thoroughly.

15 Separate the base from the scrap block along the line of the cardboard by striking it smartly with the chisel, the bevel at the tip facing towards the scrap block. The two parts will separate easily, and traces of cardboard can be removed from the underside of the base with sandpaper.

16 Mix a small quantity of wood glue and mount the lighthouse in the base, wiping away excess glue with a damp rag.

17 Finish off the wood with an application of teak oil or a polish.

18 Cut a circle of green felt and stick it to the underside of the base with adhesive.

questions

(a) What precautions must you always take to prevent personal injury from occurring whilst using the lathe? Make a list, and explain the particular danger for which you take each precaution.

(b) In roughing out the cylinder for the lighthouse (Paragraph 3), why is the best result always achieved by using the carving rather than the scraping action of the gouge?

(c) What is the main difference between roughing out a cylinder as with the lighthouse, and roughing out face-plate work, as with the base? Which is easier?

exercises

(i) There are many items you can turn on the lathe. Using the lighthouse design as a starting point, alter its proportions to make a windmill. The sails can be made easily from scrap wood.

(ii) In the illustrated example of the lighthouse, you only had to copy roughly the shape and proportions. Make a card template of the design, and turn the wood to match exactly the cut-out shape.

project 10
the garden chair

This folding canvas-seat garden chair is ideal for relaxing in the summer sunshine. You may even recognise it as a 'Director's Chair', the sort that the film industry uses when on location. It is one of the most practical of outdoor chairs, because if the two sides are detached from the seat, you have a folding lightweight fishing stool.

FIGURE 10.1

how it is designed

One of the most obvious points in favour of this chair is that it is not difficult to build, even if it looks hard. This is because the woodworking joints are confined to the mortise and tenon and the dowelled joint.

The two sides are identical in every respect (Figure 10.2), and these are made and assembled first of all. Next comes the folding stool (Figure 10.3), and when this is complete it is fitted in between the sides with hinges and metal brackets. If you want to remove the stool from the chair and use it separately, you can fix the hinges with detachable nuts and bolts instead of permanent rivets.

The seat and the chair back are made from canvas deckchair material, available either in plain or striped patterns from fabric shops.

The framework of the chair should be made from a hardwood, such as iroko or sapele. Beech is another good alternative.

tool list

Pencil	hacksaw	4 mm twist drill	bradawl
ruler	13 mm bevel chisel	2 mm twist drill	hammer
square	mallet	no. 8 wood drill	screwdriver
mortise gauge	handbrace with	countersink	file
tenon saw	16 mm centre bit	plane	lathe

cutting list

Item	Long mm	Wide mm	Thick mm
4 legs	677 (660)	35	22
2 armrests	493 (476)	45	22
2 backrests	533	35	22
2 rails	390 (356)	32	22
4 stool legs	633 (616)	32	16
2 stool rails	432	35	25

	Long mm	Diameter mm
6 side bars	380	16
1 long stool crossbar	352	16
1 short stool crossbar	312	16

Note: The figures in brackets above refer to lengths minus tenons.

how to make it

1   Begin by making the two sides of the chair (Figure 10.2). All the required lengths should be measured in pairs to ensure that they are equal — for instance, place the two armrests together side by side for marking, and do the same for all the other pieces. Then square off and cut up into individual lengths.

2   Place all four leg pieces together and mark in the mortises for the lower rail. The width of the mortise should equal approximately one-third the width of the piece in which it is being cut, and three-quarters the depth, making it a stopped mortise.

3   Adjust the pointers of the mortise gauge to 13 mm and slide the fence to a position where the pointers score

FIGURE 10.2 ELEVATION OF SIDE MEMBER

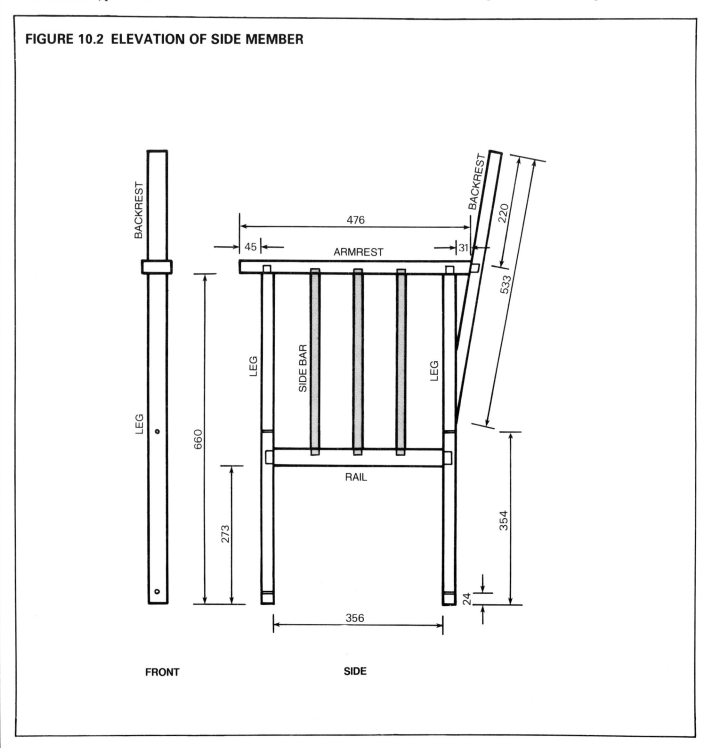

FRONT   SIDE

the leg pieces centrally across their width. Mark out the mortise, and set it in by 2 mm from each end along its length to allow for the four-shouldered tenon (Figure 10.4).

4 Taking each leg in turn, chop out the mortises using the 13 mm chisel and the mallet, cutting to a depth of 17 mm.

5 When the mortises are complete, measure for the tenons at both ends of the rail. Using the mortise gauge still set to 13 mm, adjust the fence to centralise the markers on the top and bottom faces of the rail and score the tenon lines.

6 Remove the main shoulders of the tenon with the tenon saw, then

mark in the narrow shoulders and saw these off as well (Figure 10.5). File the tenon to a smooth finish, and tap it gently into the mortise to test that it fits properly.

7 Taking the armrest, mark the two mortises in the positions shown in the side elevation (Figure 10.2). One is set in 45 mm from the front, the other

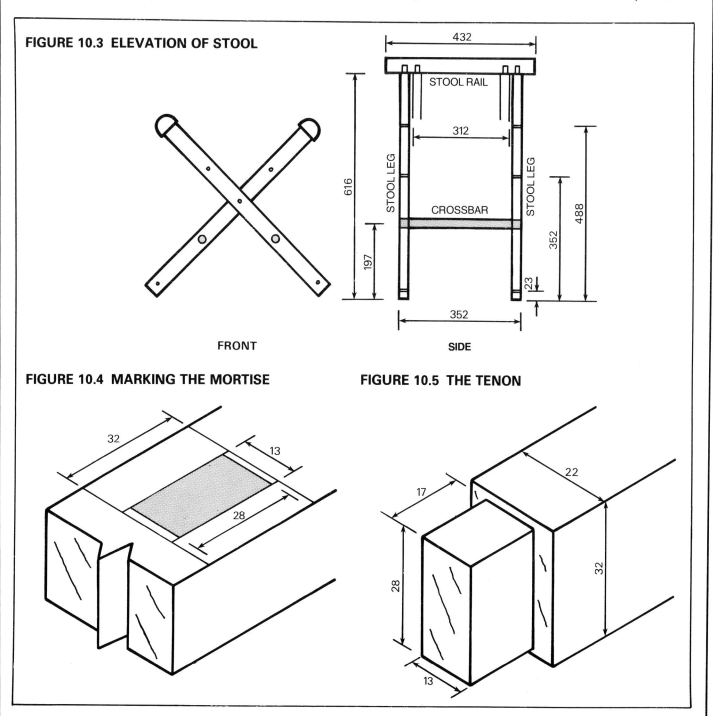

FIGURE 10.3 ELEVATION OF STOOL

FRONT

SIDE

FIGURE 10.4 MARKING THE MORTISE

FIGURE 10.5 THE TENON

31 mm from the back, excluding the armrest tenon. Keep the mortise width to 13 mm despite the additional width of the armrest. Chop out the mortises, then mark and cut corresponding tenons from the top of both leg pieces. Tap all the joints together, but do not glue them yet.

8   Measure and cut the backrest, which requires a specially-angled mortise to match the projection of the armrest at the rear. The tenon that is cut in the armrest must be similarly angled (Figure 10.6), and a wedge is cut from the bottom of the backrest to give an angle of 10°. This is best done by marking and cutting out the 10° wedge first, then laying the backrest in position against the side assembly and marking in the angle of the mortise and tenon.

9   The wedge will eventually be screwed to the leg, so drill and countersink a hole using the no. 8 bit, boring through the wedge into the leg.

10   Round off the front end of each armrest and the top end of each backrest. The lid of an aerosol can is ideal for this purpose, marking the curve around it in pencil (Figure 10.7). Remove the waste using the hacksaw and plane.

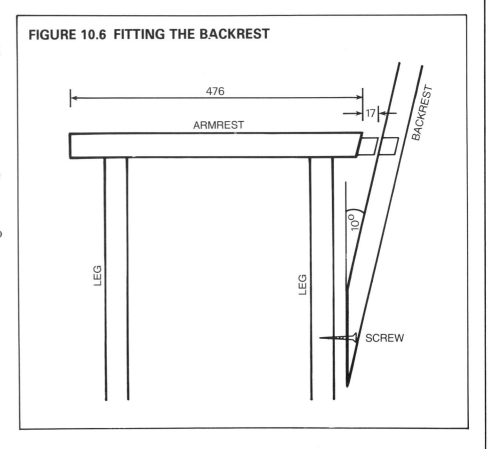

FIGURE 10.6 FITTING THE BACKREST

476

17

ARMREST

BACKREST

LEG

LEG

10°

SCREW

FIGURE 10.7

11   Measure and mark in the positions of the three side bars between the armrest and the lower rail. These bars are cut from 16 mm diameter dowelling. Their receiver holes are spaced at equal intervals

and drilled out with the 16 mm centre bit mounted in the handbrace. Each hole should be about 6-8 mm in depth. Cut the bars to length and fit them in place.

12   The stool comes next. Note that it is made in two parts with a slight difference in the position of the legs to permit both halves to be hinged. Measure and mark two mortises on the underside of each stool rail, following the positions shown in Figure 10.3, and chop these out. Mark the tenons in the top of each leg, and fit the joints together.

13   Drill out 16 mm diameter holes in the stool legs to take the crossbars, and cut the crossbars from dowelling.

14   Measure and drill the rivet holes in each of the four upright legs and the stool legs, copying the pattern of holes given in Figures 10.2 and 10.3. Mark them in with the bradawl, then use the handbrace fitted with the 4 mm twist drill to bore them out, taking suitable precautions.

15   Next, lightly plane all the pieces to round off the edges, finishing by rubbing down with fine-grade sandpaper.

16   The three parts of the chair are now ready for assembly. The joints are best put together with glue and screws for maximum rigidity, using wood glue and 25 mm by 2 mm brass screws.

17   The process of screwing up a mortise and tenon joint is known as draw-boring: first the mortise is drilled through the side with the 2 mm twist drill and countersunk, then the tenon is drilled through in a slightly offset position so that the screw pulls the joint more tightly together.

18   When the backrest is fitted in position, screw the wedge down with a no. 8 brass screw.

19   If you want a detachable fishing stool, hinge the chair together with galvanised nuts and bolts; otherwise a more permanent arrangement should be made using flat-headed mild steel

FIGURE 10.8

nails (Figure 10.8). These are turned into simple rivets by sawing the ends off and tapping the sawn end with a hammer to squash out a new head — taking care to avoid denting the wood. Plain washers and a thin rubber washer form the remaining parts of the hinge (Figure 10.9).

20 Where the legs of the stool are hinged to the side legs, two wooden spacer blocks are required to take up the gaps. Their dimensions are shown in Figure 10.10, and they can be run off easily on the lathe. Drill a 4 mm hole through their centres.

21 The metal stay brackets are cut from strip metal not less than 2 mm thick. There are four brackets holding the stool to the sides. Two of these remain straight, but the other two are bent to the shape shown in Figure 10.11.

22 You must decide for yourself how far apart to drill the holes in the metal, referring to the dimensions for guidance only. The idea is that when fitted, the brackets should permit the chair to fold up easily, and when unfolded, the stool should not come into contact with the sides but stand off by about 5 mm.

23 The wood may be either stained or painted. If it is stained, finish with a suitable furniture polish. Do not varnish, because this will only rub away from the hinged joints.

24 The material for the chair and seat-back is canvas, available from fabric shops. As this is not part of the woodwork, you will have to make these in your spare time. Stitch a 12 mm hem all around both pieces of material, and remember to allow sufficient width to tuck the hemmed sides underneath the stool and around the backrests before finally tacking in position with dome-headed brass tacks.

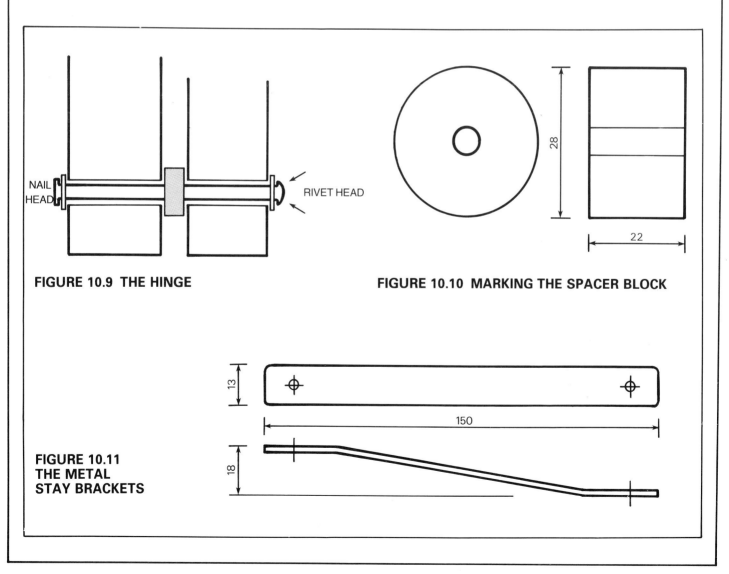

FIGURE 10.9 THE HINGE

NAIL HEAD

RIVET HEAD

FIGURE 10.10 MARKING THE SPACER BLOCK

28

22

FIGURE 10.11 THE METAL STAY BRACKETS

13

150

18

questions

(a)   In selecting a suitable hardwood for this project, what particular qualities must you look for? And what must you avoid?

(b)   When chopping out mortises that sink three-quarters of the way into the wood (Paragraphs 4 and 7), how do you prevent the chisel from splitting right through?

(c)   For the three parts of the chair to fit together properly, the rivet holes must be measured and drilled with great accuracy (Paragraph 14). How is this best achieved?

(d)   Why is draw-boring an essential part of assembling the mortise and tenon joints?

exercises

(I)   The deck chair and footrest is another type of garden chair. Working from the example shown in Figure 10.12, draw up a design for your own deck chair. Note that the armrests are hinged to fold flat, and the footrest is a modified version of the picnic table. Make use of this fact in your design.

FIGURE 10.12

(II)   Create an outdoor chair of your own to suit a particular purpose: for example, a simple folding picnic chair, or a long reclining sunbed, etc.

(III)   Work out the cost of making the garden chair, or deck chair, etc, using different types of wood, such as the options like iroko and beech, already mentioned.

project 11
the table tennis table

The size of our table tennis table is 2180 mm by 1260mm, which is less than three-quarters the size of a standard table. Its top surface is 760 mm off the ground, and this is the regulation height. It folds in half and the four pairs of legs are hinged to allow for easy storage. It is an ideal table for playing table tennis either indoors or outside in the open air.

FIGURE 11.1

how it is designed

The 'three-quarter' size is convenient because it saves on timber, which means also that the table is lighter and easier to carry around. In addition, the plywood top surface can be cut from a single sheet measuring 2440mm by 1220mm, the standard size for ply.

Two types of joint are used in the construction of the table frame and leg assemblies: the mitre and the halved joint. Both of these are comparatively simple joints, but they

must be measured and cut accurately.

The table top is built in two identical halves which are hinged together along the net-line with three butt hinges (Figure 11.2). Each half section has two identical pairs of hinged legs which fold inwards and overlap as they lie flat against the underside of the table. One of these pairs is shown in Figure 11.3. The leg assemblies are each joined to the table frame by two backflap hinges and one collapsible stay or bracket (Figure 11.4).

The table frame and legs are built from softwood, pine or red deal being suitable. Taking the two halves of the table separately, each of the four main side members is rebated to a depth of 9mm, equal to the thickness of the plywood covering material. It is best to use birch-faced ply.

Hardwood could be used for the frame, but this will make the table substantially heavier and more expensive, unless you select one of the cheaper and less dense woods such as agba or obeche.

FIGURE 11.2 PLAN OF TABLE

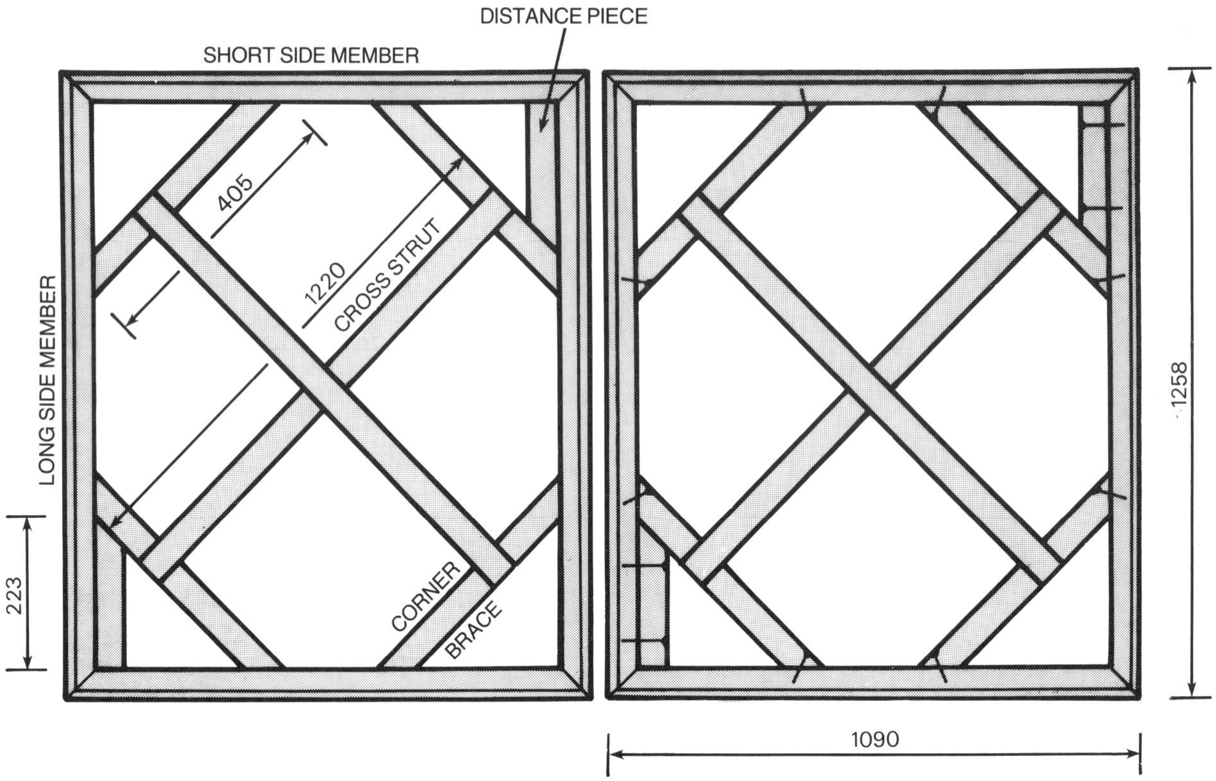

DISTANCE PIECE

SHORT SIDE MEMBER

LONG SIDE MEMBER

405

1220

CROSS STRUT

223

CORNER

BRACE

1258

1090

**FIGURE 11.3
ELEVATION OF LEG ASSEMBLY**

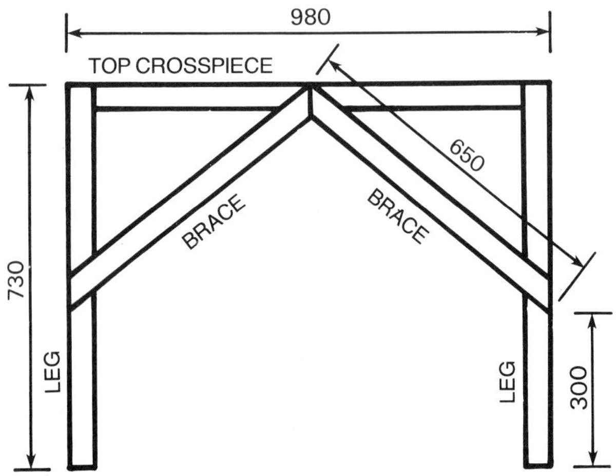

980

TOP CROSSPIECE

650

BRACE

BRACE

730

LEG

LEG

300

**FIGURE 11.4
COLLAPSIBLE BRACKET ARRANGEMENT**

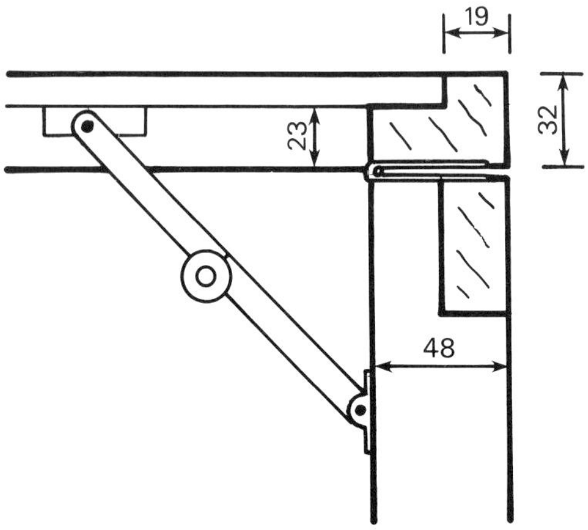

19

23

32

48

tool list

Pencil
ruler
square
marking gauge
tenon saw
handsaw
19 mm bevel chisel
mallet
handbrace with no. 8 wood drill
countersink
plane
plough plane
bradawl
screwdriver
hammer
file
mitre box

cutting list

Item	Long mm	Wide mm	Thick mm
4 long rebated side members	1258	48	32
4 short rebated side members	1090	48	32
8 corner braces	405	48	23
4 cross struts	1220	48	23
4 distance pieces	223	48	23
8 legs	730	48	48
4 top crosspieces	980	48	48
8 leg braces	650	48	23
2 plywood top surface panels	1220	1052	9

how to make it

1 Prepare rebates in the lengths to be used for the side members, using the plough plane with a suitable cutter. The rebates are cut in the top face, and measure 29 mm in width and 9 mm in depth (Figure 11.5).

2 Measure out all the side members, marking the lengths with the square and pencil. Taking the pieces one by one, place them in the mitre box and cut the mitres using the tenon saw (Figure 11.6). Run the saw smoothly in the slot, avoiding fierce jerky movements.

FIGURE 11.6

3 Taking the two half-sections of the table individually, cut the four side members for one half. Arrange

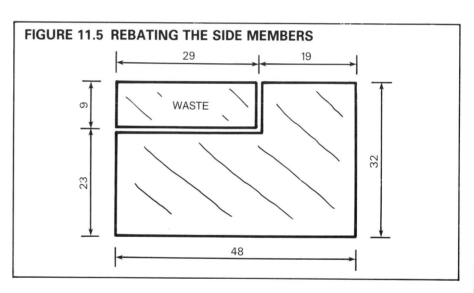

FIGURE 11.5 REBATING THE SIDE MEMBERS

these together on a flat floor surface to check that the mitres all fit accurately.

4 Measure the four corner braces to a length of 405 mm each and cut a mitre at either end. Note that the wood used for these braces is 23 mm thick to enable it to lie flush with the rebates cut in the side members. Position the braces one in each corner.

5 Next, measure and cut the two distance pieces with a mitre at one end and a right-angled cut at the

other end, giving a maximum length of 223 mm. These are fitted into place in diagonally opposite corners, as shown in Figure 11.2, to allow for the eventual attachment of the leg assemblies, which must be offset from one another to permit them to overlap as they fold flat.

6 Lay the cross struts in position on the braces one at a time, checking with the square that they rest at 90° — their position is not critical — and mark them on the braces with the square and pencil. Each of the cross struts is fitted to its two braces with a halved joint (Figure 11.7), and the same joint is used to fit both the struts together at the point in the centre where they cross.

7 Mark out all the halved joints using the marking gauge with its pointer set to half the thickness of the wood. To remove the waste from the braces, clamp each piece in the vice and make a series of cuts with the tenon saw down as far as the depth line. Chop out the waste with the 19 mm chisel, and file smooth.

8 Remove the waste from the ends of the cross struts using the tenon saw. Finally prepare the single halved joint at the centre of the struts using the same method as for the braces.

9 Drill and countersink holes through each of the halved joints to take 19 mm no. 8 screws. Following the screw directions shown on the right-hand side of Figure 11.2, drill holes in the braces and distance pieces with the no. 8 bit, once again countersinking for the screwheads. The braces are fixed to the side members with 50 mm screws, and 75 mm screws are used for the distance pieces.

10 Mark and drill the corresponding screw positions in the side members and assemble the frame (Figure 11.8), but do not glue it together yet. Repeat the same procedure for the second half of the table, which is identical in every respect.

FIGURE 11.8

11 The four leg assemblies are made next. These are identical in shape and size. The legs and top crosspieces are cut from 48 mm

FIGURE 11.7 THE HALVED JOINT

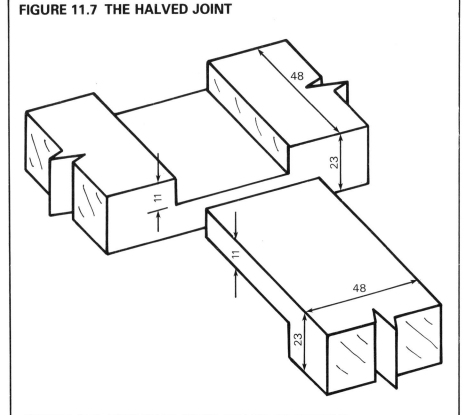

FIGURE 11.9 EXPLODED VIEW OF LEG ASSEMBLY

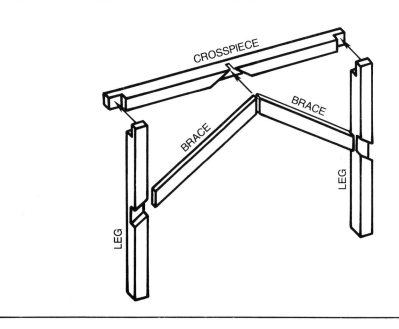

square wood whilst the braces are 48 mm by 23 mm. Halved joints are used to join the two legs to each crosspiece. They must fit exactly at right-angles. The two braces fit into

slots which are cut to a depth of 23 mm to match their thickness, and meet at the centre of the crosspiece in a triangular housing cut to the same depth (Figure 11.9).

12 Drill and countersink a single no. 8 screw hole into each joint to take a 38 mm screw. Mix a quantity of wood glue, and apply it to all of the joints, screwing them fully home. When the glue has set hard, trim off any projections with the plane.

13 When all the four leg assemblies are complete, they are each joined to the underside of the table frame by two 38 mm backflap hinges. These are positioned in such a way that the two pairs of leg assemblies on each frame fold flat with the legs lying side by side. The distance pieces allow for this to happen.

14 Mark out a rebate for each hinge 75 mm from the ends of the leg crosspieces and chisel out a shallow recess. Screw the hinges in place, then bring the leg assembly up to the table frame and mark in the hinge positions, rebating similarly.

15 The collapsible stays or brackets hold the legs securely when the table is standing: they have a knuckle joint at the centre and hinged fixing plates at either end. They come in various sizes, but the type used here measures 100 mm when folded.

16 With the aid of a 45° set-square, place each bracket in position and mark the hinge plate with the bradawl. Then fold the legs flat and check that the markings still line up when the bracket is fully closed. The hinge-and-bracket arrangement is shown is Figure 11.4.

17 Dismantle the table frame and attach the brackets with thin countersunk 19 mm screws to the side member and the distance piece. When the brackets are in position mix more glue and assemble the table joints with glue and screws.

FIGURE 11.10

18 Drive nails into the mitres to hold them firmly together. Screw the collapsible brackets to the legs (Figure 11.10).

19 Hinge both the table halves together with three 75 mm butt hinges, suitably recessed with the top of the hinge knuckles lying flush with the surface of the table. Drill out the screw holes and attach the hinges with 38 mm no. 8 wood screws.

20 Cut and plane the two plywood top surfaces exactly to size so that they drop into the rebates and fit perfectly. Mix a further quantity of wood glue and brush it into the rebates and onto the braces and cross struts. Fix the plywood in position and fasten it down with veneer pins driven through into the rebates and struts.

21 When the glue has set hard, rub down all the surfaces thoroughly with medium-grade and then fine-grade sandpaper.

22 The table is painted, the usual colour being a matt dark green playing surface with white lines running around the outside edges of the table top measuring 19 mm in width, and a white line down the centre 3 mm in width to mark out the doubles service areas. Finish with a matt varnish.

questions

(a) Why are the side members all rebated, when the two plywood top surfaces could just as easily have been extended to cover the entire table top?

(b) What is the main purpose of the cross struts? Do they merely act as additional supports for the plywood top surface?

(c) Why are you told in Paragraph 10 to assemble the table frame with screws but not to make the assembly permanent yet with glue?

(d) Why must the dark green paint and the varnish for the playing surface be matt (Paragraph 22)? And what is the best way of painting on straight white lines?

(e) The best way of keeping the legs and the two table halves folded up for transport and storage is by securing them with clips or catches. What sort of catches are the most suitable, and where would you put them?

exercises

(i) Draw up plans for a full-sized table tennis table, measuring 2740 mm by 1525 mm, with the top surface 760 mm off the ground. Bearing in mind that plywood is sold in sheets of 2440 mm by 1220 mm, how will you arrange your top surfaces? Will it mean altering the positions of the cross struts, or adding to them with extra struts? If so, why?

(ii) Imagine that you want to keep to the three-quarter size table, but use a thicker plywood, such as 13 mm, instead of 9 mm. Make appropriate alterations to the wood sizes shown in the cutting list. Will your new table inevitably be heavier?

(iii) It is obvious that the complete table tennis table is made up of two identical halves which could easily exist on their own. Think of other purposes for which you could adapt the basic design. It does not have to be for a sports table of any kind.

project 12
the bathroom cabinet

A simple cabinet with a middle shelf and sliding mirror doors is often all that you need in the bathroom to store medicines, soaps and hair shampoo. It is fixed to the wall with two screws.

FIGURE 12.1

how it is designed

The cabinet is made in the form of a box-type carcase with a top, a bottom and two side pieces. A panel of white-surfaced hardboard is fitted in a groove at the back that runs all around the inside faces of the box. A middle shelf is mounted inside the cabinet.

The two sliding mirror doors and their double-channel running track are not shown in Figure 12.2 to avoid confusion.

The joints used in the cabinet's construction are the dovetail joint used to fit the four corners together; the housing joint securing the back panel into its four grooves; and the dowelled joint attaching the middle shelf in position.

The recommended wood is Parana pine, a light-coloured softwood. It is silky to the touch, free of knots, straight-grained and good to work with. Alternatively you could use white pine or Brazilian mahogany.

tool list

Pencil	tenon saw	handbrace with 9 mm twist drill
ruler	13 mm bevel chisel	and no. 8 wood drill
square	mallet	plane
		plough plane with 5 mm cutter

cutting list

Item	Long mm	Wide mm	Thick mm
1 top and 1 bottom piece	470	150	17
2 side pieces	350	150	17
1 middle shelf	435	115	17

	Long mm	Diameter mm	
4 dowel pegs	25	9	

1 sheet of 4 mm-thick white-surfaced hardboard measuring 443 mm by 323 mm

Note: The grain runs along the length of each piece.

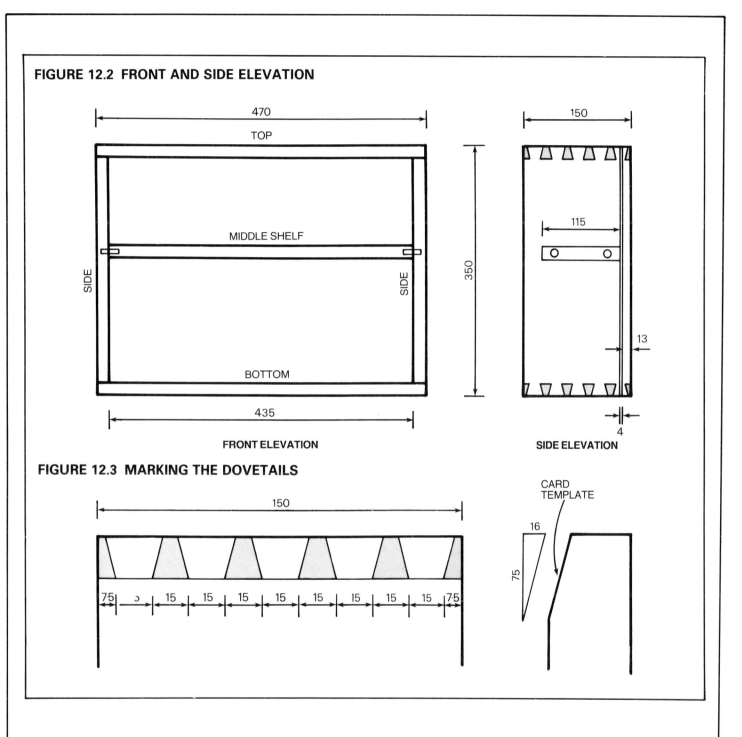

FIGURE 12.2 FRONT AND SIDE ELEVATION

470

TOP

150

MIDDLE SHELF

350

SIDE

SIDE

115

BOTTOM

435

13

FRONT ELEVATION

4

SIDE ELEVATION

FIGURE 12.3 MARKING THE DOVETAILS

150

CARD
TEMPLATE

16

75

7.5 5 15 15 15 15 15 15 15 15 7.5

how to make it

1 Cut and plane the five pieces to size, ensuring that all the ends are exactly square.

2 Mark in the dovetail joints, noting that the dovetails are cut in the side pieces and the receiver slots cut in the top and bottom lengths (Figure 12.2).

3 Our example has five dovetails per joint, each with a width of 15mm at the narrowest part, and each separated by 15mm from its neighbour. The two end dovetails are set in by half of this amount, or 7.5mm, from both edges, so that the whole arrangement fits neatly into the 150mm-width of the wood (Figure 12.3). Use a card template to set the correct gradient, and complete

the marking by joining up with squared pencil lines on the end-grain.

4 Clamp the dovetail piece vertically in the vice and saw on the waste side of all the lines with the tenon saw, taking the cuts down as far as the shoulder line.

5 When all the saw-cuts are complete, transfer the dovetail positions onto the end of the receiver

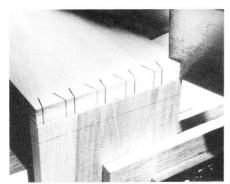

FIGURE 12.4

piece to show where the sockets are to be cut. The dovetail pattern is made by holding the two pieces firmly together at right-angles, and drawing the tenon saw very carefully through the kerf to make a mark (Figure 12.4).

6 With the pencil and ruler, mark in the position of the sockets between all the kerf cuts and the shoulder line. Then place the piece upright in the vice and saw down to the line, working the saw once again on the waste side of the marking.

7 When all the sawing is complete, chop out the waste from between the dovetails with the 13 mm chisel and mallet. Firstly work the chisel until the blade passes halfway through the thickness of the piece, then turn it over and chop from the other side until the chisel cuts meet and the waste can be removed.

8 Remove the two narrow waste pieces from the extreme edges of the dovetails with the tenon saw.

9 Chop out the waste from between the sockets, using the same method as before except that the chisel must be held at a sideways angle to follow the slope of the sockets.

10 The completed dovetail joint (Figure 12.5) should not be fitted together experimentally, unlike most other types of joint, because it will be difficult to separate the two parts of the joint again without loosening or splitting the wood. The most you can do is hold the dovetails against the sockets to check that the slopes match perfectly.

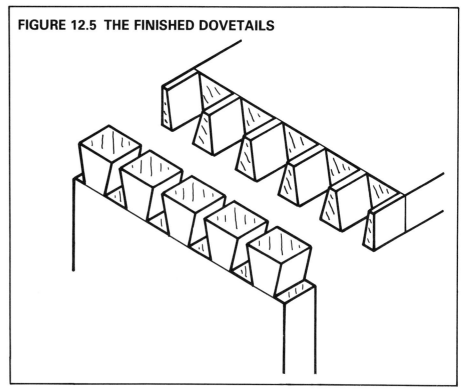

FIGURE 12.5 THE FINISHED DOVETAILS

11 The next task is to cut the grooves for the back panel in the top, bottom and two side pieces, using the plough plane. Fit the plough with the 5 mm cutter, then adjust the depth gauge to cut a groove 5 mm deep and set the fence so that the groove is placed 13 mm from the rear edge. Plane out a groove in each of the four pieces, cutting along the whole length (Figure 12.6).

FIGURE 12.6

12 Cut the back panel from the sheet of hardboard, allowing 4 mm to fit into the groove. This is marginally less than the 5 mm depth of the groove, a gap which will be taken up if the wood shrinks.

13 Drill two holes in the upper part of the hardboard for the wall-fixing screws: the position of these holes is not critical, but should be approximately 75 mm from the sides and 60 mm down from the top.

14 Take the middle shelf and drill out two 9 mm diameter holes at either end to a depth of 16 mm. Cut four lengths of dowelling each measuring 25 mm, and glue these into the holes, leaving 9 mm projecting.

15 Measure and drill out corresponding receiver holes on the inner faces of the two side pieces, setting the shelf back against the groove. The position of the shelf within the cabinet does not have to be exactly halfway up. It could, for example, go slightly higher to permit the storage of larger bottles and items on the bottom shelf.

16 Mix more wood glue and assemble the cabinet. Begin by tapping the top and bottom pieces and the middle shelf into one of the side pieces, making sure all the joints go fully home, then slide the back panel into its grooves and finally place the second side piece in position. Clamp the assembly together and wipe away excess glue.

17   Four square holes are visible, where the plough plane has cut its grooves through the dovetails, one at each corner. Cut short lengths of 5 mm square scrap woodstrip and glue them in to plug the holes (Figure 12.7).

18   When the glue has set hard, rub down the joints with fine sandpaper. The cabinet can now be painted or stained, whichever you prefer, or left in its natural wood colour with a coat of clear varnish.

19   The cabinet is finished off by fitting sliding mirror doors. These are mounted in running track, which comes in two sizes. The upper track is

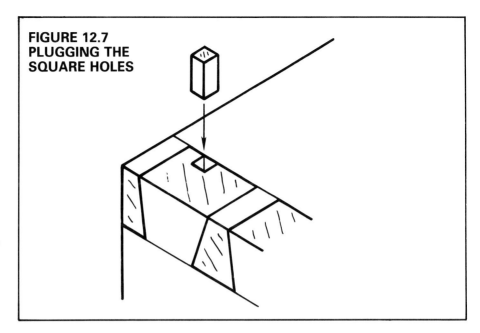

FIGURE 12.7 PLUGGING THE SQUARE HOLES

deeper than the lower one. Cut both lengths to size and fix them in position with strong adhesive. The

two mirror doors must be measured accurately and ordered from your local glass supplier.

questions

(a)   Most factory-manufactured bathroom cabinets are made of melamine, which is chipboard covered in white plastic veneer. What are the reasons for using Parana pine instead of melamine? Is it possible to cut dovetail joints in chipboard?

(b)   What precautions must you take when planing the five pieces to size (Paragraph 1)?

(c)   Why is it an important feature of the cabinet that the dovetails are cut in the two side pieces? Would it make any difference if they were cut in the top and bottom pieces instead? Think carefully about the construction of the cabinet, the weight of its contents and the way it is secured to the wall.

(d)   The gradient of each dovetail is marked using a card template (Paragraph 3 and Figure 12.3). The gradient should not be too great, nor too shallow. Why?

(e)   The best way of using the plough plane is to begin planing at the far end and gradually work backwards, increasing the length of the strokes all the time. What is the reason for this?

(f)   Having completed the cabinet, how would you fix it to the bathroom wall? Give full details.

exercises

(i)   Adapt the design of the cabinet to produce a larger example, with an additional open bottom shelf not enclosed by sliding mirror doors.

(ii)   Suppose that you have been asked to make a bathroom cabinet like this one, but without sliding mirror doors. Instead, you are to fit plain hinged wooden doors. Plan the necessary modifications, remembering that you will need more wood for the doors. Include the extra wood in your revised cutting list.

(iii)   A cabinet like this could be used for a variety of purposes; it does not only have to be for the bathroom. Making slight alterations where necessary, think up an alternative use for it. Try changing the overall dimensions, do away with the middle shelf, etc.

(iv)   Work out the difference in the cost of making the cabinet in Parana pine, compared with making it in white pine or Brazilian mahogany.

project 13
the bedside cabinet

In order to serve a useful purpose, the bedside cabinet does not need to be an elaborate piece of furniture with drawers and cupboards. The type of cabinet in our example has enough storage space to accommodate all the usual items: clock, lamp, radio, books and magazines.

how it is designed

The framework of the cabinet is designed on the stool-construction principle (Figures 13.2 and 13.3 — the shaded parts), where four corner posts are joined by top, mid and bottom rails which not only make for a rigid structure but also act as supports for the three shelves. The shelves are cut from plywood sheet, as are the side and back panels.

The frame is put together with mortise and tenon joints throughout, all the tenons being of the four-shouldered variety. The top shelf is screwed in place, whilst the other two shelves and the side and back panels are glued and tacked onto the frame.

The wood used for the framework is beech, which is an ideal hardwood for this sort of work. Other hardwoods could be used instead, like sycamore which is also light in colour; both of these woods will match well with the plywood if the finished cabinet is not to be stained. The plywood is birch-faced, which has a good quality surface suitable for this type of interior furniture.

tool list

Pencil
ruler
square
mortise gauge
tenon saw
handsaw
6 mm bevel chisel
19 mm bevel chisel
mallet
handbrace with no. 8 wood drill
countersink
plane
spokeshave
bradawl
hammer
cross-head screwdriver
file

FIGURE 13.1

cutting list

Item	Long mm	Wide mm	Thick mm
4 posts	540	28	22
2 long top rails	475 (451)	22	16
2 short top rails	368 (344)	22	16
2 long mid rails	475 (451)	16	16
2 short mid rails	368 (344)	16	16
2 long bottom rails	475 (451)	48	16
2 short bottom rails	368 (344)	48	16
1 top shelf	600	460	13
1 mid and 1 bottom shelf	495	400	13
2 side panels	540	406	6
1 back panel	540	495	6

Note: The figures in brackets above refer to rail lengths minus tenons.

The grain runs along the length of each piece.

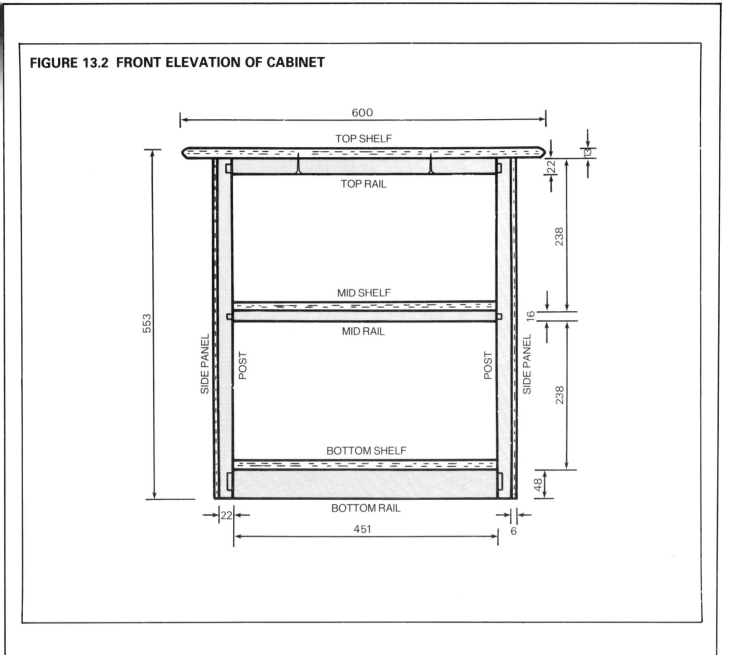

FIGURE 13.2 FRONT ELEVATION OF CABINET

600

TOP SHELF

13

22

TOP RAIL

238

MID SHELF

16

MID RAIL

238

553

SIDE PANEL

POST

POST

SIDE PANEL

BOTTOM SHELF

48

BOTTOM RAIL

22

451

6

how to make it

1 Cut and plane the four corner posts to size, marking them deliberately with an excess of wood at both ends. This will be trimmed at a later stage, but for the moment it helps to prevent the top and bottom mortises from splitting the wood as they are being cut, since they are positioned very close to the finished ends.

2 Before marking in the various positions of the mortises, note that the rails all have a common thickness but a variety of widths. From Figures 13.2 and 13.3 you can see that the top, mid and bottom rails are 22 mm, 16 mm, and 48 mm wide respectively. All the rails are 16 mm thick.

3 Measure and mark out all the mortises. Note first of all, though, that both faces of the post are unequal to the thickness of each rail (Figure 13.4 inset and Figure 13.5). Following the one-third rule in setting the mortise gauge, adjust the pointers of the gauge to one-third the thickness of the rail, which is approximately 6 mm. Set the fence of

the gauge so that the pointers score each rail centrally along the 16 mm thickness face.

4 Mark in the position of each mortise on all four posts, placing them at the specified height. Scribe the mortise lines with the gauge, always running the fence of the gauge along the outside faces of the posts to set the lines in their correct positions as shown in Figure 13.4.

5 Set in the mortises at top and bottom by the following amounts: for the top rail, set in by 6 mm at the top and 2 mm at the bottom; for the mid rail, 2 mm top and bottom; for the bottom rail, 2 mm at the top and 15 mm at the bottom. All the mortises should be cut to a depth of 12 mm.

6 Taking each post in turn, clamp the piece in the vice and chop out the mortises with the 6 mm chisel and the mallet. Start in the middle of the marked area and work gradually outwards in the direction of the grain.

7 When all the mortises are complete, the next stage is to measure and cut the tenons at each end of the twelve rails. Without altering the setting of the mortise gauge, mark the tenons to a depth of 12 mm to match the mortises. Because the mortises have been set in, the tenons will be cut with four shoulders (Figure 13.6). Remove the shoulders with the tenon saw, and finish off with the file. Fit the tenon into the mortise, tapping it gently home with the mallet.

8 When all the joints are complete, assemble the whole framework experimentally without glue to check that each joint fits soundly home and that the corners form perfect right-angles. Then dismantle the framework.

9 Take the four top rails and measure each one in turn to take two screw-holes. These screws are for securing the plywood top shelf, and each screw is placed halfway between the midpoint and the end of the rail (Figures 13.2 and 13.3).

10 Clamp the rail upside-down in the vice and drill through with the no. 8 wood drill mounted in the handbrace. Stand the square near the hole to line up the handbrace and keep it drilling vertically. Countersink each hole.

11 Mix a quantity of wood glue and assemble the front and back components of the framework. In each case, fit the three rails to the two posts. Check with the square that all the joints form right-angles, and then cramp up the assembly and place to one side until the glue has set hard.

12 Dismantle the cramps and trim the excess wood from both ends of the

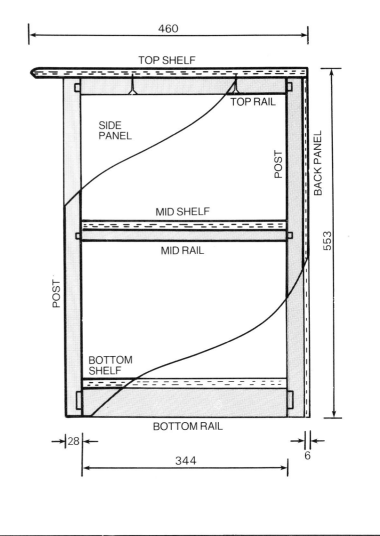

FIGURE 13.3. SIDE ELEVATION OF CABINET

460

TOP SHELF

TOP RAIL

SIDE PANEL

POST

BACK PANEL

MID SHELF

MID RAIL

553

POST

BOTTOM SHELF

BOTTOM RAIL

28

344

6

posts, using the tenon saw with the assembly held in the vice.

13 Measure and cut the mid and bottom shelves to size, using the handsaw. The grain direction can be seen quite easily on the surface of the ply, and the shelves should be cut with the grain running from one side of the cabinet to the other. Cut small rectangular pieces from each corner to fit around the posts (Figure 13.7).

14 Repeat the gluing procedure for the two sets of side rails, to join up the front section of the framework to the back. Before knocking the joints fully

home, fit the shelves into position (Figure 13.8), and then complete the assembly of the joints, cramping them up tightly. The reason for

FIGURE 13.8

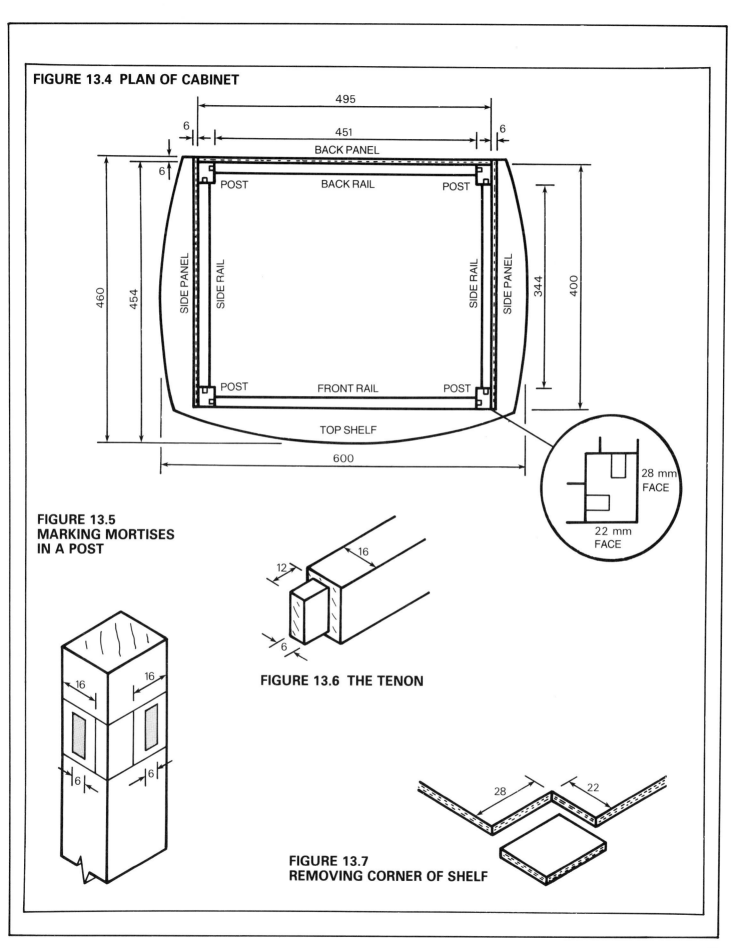

FIGURE 13.4 PLAN OF CABINET

495
6
451
6
6
BACK PANEL
POST
BACK RAIL
POST
SIDE PANEL
SIDE RAIL
SIDE RAIL
SIDE PANEL
460
454
344
400
POST
FRONT RAIL
POST
TOP SHELF
600

28 mm
FACE
22 mm
FACE

**FIGURE 13.5
MARKING MORTISES
IN A POST**

16
16
6
6

16

12
16
6

FIGURE 13.6 THE TENON

28
22

**FIGURE 13.7
REMOVING CORNER OF SHELF**

67

putting the shelves in position loose is that they will not slide into the framework once it has been fully assembled.

15 When the glue has set hard, remove the cramps. Mix fresh glue and apply it between the shelves and their supporting rails, securing them with two panel pins along each side.

16 Measure and cut the top shelf to size. As this is such a prominent part of the cabinet it is given a gentle curve on its front and side edges to make it look more 'finished' and attractive.

17 To draw these curved lines, make a simple compass by taking a long piece of hardwood batten, 25 mm by 13 mm material, and hammer a panel pin through one end to act as a pivot. Drill two 6 mm diameter holes at the other end, one of them located 800 mm and the other 900 mm from the pivot. Place a pencil through the 800 mm radius hole and mark in the side curves on the plywood, and draw in the 900 mm radius arc on the front edge (Figure 13.9). Before cutting, check that all the corners lie outside the framework.

18 Saw off the waste plywood using the handsaw, then place the piece in the vice and plane off the remaining waste with the spokeshave (Figure 13.10). Chamfer the front and side

FIGURE 13.10

edges to round them off, following the pattern shown in Figure 13.11. Finish by rubbing down with medium-grade and then fine sandpaper, smoothing the edges and corners.

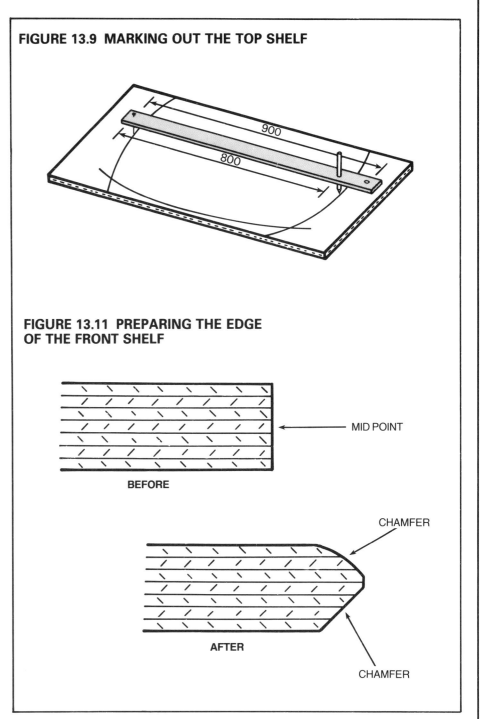

FIGURE 13.9 MARKING OUT THE TOP SHELF

900

800

FIGURE 13.11 PREPARING THE EDGE OF THE FRONT SHELF

MID POINT

BEFORE

CHAMFER

CHAMFER

AFTER

19 Place the top shelf upside-down on a flat surface and position the inverted framework onto it in its correct position, allowing an overhang of 6 mm at the back for the plywood rear panel to be fitted flush with the rear edge. Mark through the eight screw-holes with the bradawl, and drill into the ply with the no. 8 bit to a depth of approximately 9 mm.

20 Brush a mixing of glue along the top of the four rails and place the shelf in position, screwing it down with galvanised 32 mm cross-head screws.

21 Starting with the back, cut the three remaining panels for the back and the two sides from 6 mm plywood, with the grain running from top to bottom, and plane down the edges until each panel fits neatly on the frame. Glue and tack the panels in place.

22 Cut lengths of rounded-section hardwood beading to cover the exposed front edge of the mid and bottom shelves, and bevel both ends of each bead with the 19 mm chisel to give a more refined finish. Fit these in position with glue and tacks (Figure 13.12).

23 Fix four 'domes of silence' to the underside, one in each post.

24 You can leave the wood in its natural colour, stain it with wood dye or paint it white. If you choose to leave the wood as it is, or stain it, finish off with at least two coats of clear varnish, preferably semi-matt.

FIGURE 13.12

questions

(a) If you could not use beech or sycamore for the frame, what other type of wood might you consider using? Is there a suitable alternative to the birch-faced ply?

(b) The four corner posts must each be squared very accurately (Paragraph 1). What method do you use for this?

(c) How do the mortise and tenon joints in this project differ from the sort that you usually encounter? What would be the most obvious problem caused by putting them in the wrong place?

(d) Why is the top shelf screwed in position, whereas the mid and bottom shelves are glued and tacked?

exercises

(i) Making suitable modifications to the design where appropriate, convert the bedside cabinet to other uses: for example, to store records.

(ii) Suppose that you want to fit two hinged doors to the cabinet. Decide what material you would use for the doors, and plan the necessary alterations.

(iii) Design a cabinet of your own, using the same materials. Try to make the design as original as you can, and remember that sometimes a cabinet is placed between two single beds.

(iv) Work out the cost of making the cabinet using beech or sycamore. Compare this with the cost of other types of wood that you might consider using instead.

project 14
the three coffee tables

Coffee tables usually come in sets of three, and are designed to fit one into another for convenient storage. Furniture of this sort should be of the highest quality, attractive in design and capable of standing up to many years' hard use.

The cost of the wood and the amount of time spent on this project may restrict you to making one table only.

how they are designed

The design chiefly makes use of curved lines for the legs, the bases and the lower back rails (Figure 14.2). The object is to produce stability, with a high proportion of the tables' weight being gathered near the base, and narrower lines at the level of the table top.

Each table is made in four stages. Firstly the two identical side sections are built; these are then fitted with two crosspieces at the top and one at the bottom. Next, the table surface groundwork is cut from plywood which fits into grooves cut in all four top rails. Finally the top surface is made up of thin wooden blocks or tiles arranged in a pattern and fitted into the recess between the plywood and the top of the table.

The table frame is assembled with mortise and tenon joints. The plywood groundwork is fitted to the frame using housing joints. The woodblocks are butted together and glued down onto the groundwork.

The three tables differ mainly in respect of their size, and both the

FIGURE 14.1

medium and small tables are constructed to fit in sequence into the large table with the minimum of clearance. The only other difference is that the large and medium tables have narrow front top rails to allow for this clearance, the smallest table having the full rail.

If you decide to make one table only, use a full front rail and add one more lower curved crosspiece to close off the opening at the front.

A good quality wood should be used to bring out the best result, such as afrormosia or Burmese teak, but

these hardwoods can be expensive. As an alternative you could use agba or Brazilian mahogany. If you are lucky you might be able to salvage old oak or mahogany from discarded furniture, such as old solid wardrobes and bed boards. This can be an excellent source of cheap high quality wood, but you will have to be persistent in your search. Schools sometimes get rid of old oak desks and classroom fittings.

The plywood for the groundwork may be ordinary ply, but the birch-faced variety is better.

tool list

Pencil	handsaw	mallet	plough plane
ruler	coping saw	handbrace with	spokeshave
square	19mm bevel chisel	4mm twist drill	file
mortise gauge	6mm bevel chisel	plane	trimming knife
tenon saw			

cutting list

LARGE TABLE

Item	Long mm	Wide mm	Thick mm
4 legs	432	100	19
2 bases	508	60	19
2 top rails	450 (432)	40	19
1 top front crosspiece	488 (470)	28	19
1 top back crosspiece	488 (470)	40	19
1 bottom back crosspiece	488 (470)	68	19
4 outer row woodblocks	372	98	9
4 middle row woodblocks	176	98	9
1 centre woodblock	78	78	9
1 plywood groundwork panel	482	482	13

MEDIUM TABLE

Item	Long mm	Wide mm	Thick mm
4 legs	394	100	19
2 bases	445	60	19
2 top rails	387 (369)	40	19
1 top front crosspiece	425 (407)	28	19
1 top back crosspiece	425 (407)	40	19
1 bottom back crosspiece	425 (407)	68	19
4 outer row woodblocks	325	82	9
4 middle row woodblocks	161	82	9
1 centre woodblock	79	79	9
1 plywood groundwork panel	419	419	13

SMALL TABLE

Item	Long mm	Wide mm	Thick mm
4 legs	356	100	19
2 bases	381	60	19
2 top rails	323 (305)	40	19
2 top crosspieces	361 (343)	40	19
1 bottom back crosspiece	361 (343)	68	19
4 outer row woodblocks	273	70	9
4 middle row woodblocks	133	70	9
1 centre woodblock	63	63	9
1 plywood groundwork panel	358	358	13

Note: The figures in brackets above refer to rail lengths minus tenons.

how to make them

1 Draw out templates for the legs, base and bottom crosspiece for each table, marking the pattern with a pencil onto thick card. The card should be pinned on a flat surface such as a drawing board and all straight lines drawn with the aid of a T-square and set squares to ensure accurate angles.

2 The legs meet the base at 90°, each leg being angled at 60° and the base at 30° (Figure 14.3). These angles must be reproduced exactly on the templates. The curves are drawn with a compass made from a length of 25 mm by 13 mm hardwood batten. Hammer in a panel pin at one end to act as a pivot, and drill a 4 mm diameter hole at the other end to take the pencil. The radii of curvature are: large table 915 mm; medium 800 mm; small 685 mm.

3 When the templates have been marked, cut them out carefully with the sharp trimming knife. Transfer them one at a time onto an appropriate section of wood, aligning the straight edge of the template with the straight edge of the wood. Stick down the template at each end with adhesive tape and draw a pencil line around it (Figure 14.4). Mark in an extra 9 mm for the tenon at the bottom of each leg, shown as the shaded area in Figure 14.3, and also at the two ends of each curved back crosspiece.

4 Cut up the wood into individual pieces with the coping saw, leaving the bulk of the waste to be removed from the curved sections with the spokeshave, and from the straight sections with the plane.

5 Starting with the legs, clamp the work in the vice and manipulate the spokeshave to remove the waste until it comes within about 2 mm of the curved pencil line (Figure 14.5). Stop at this point. Then, when all four leg sections have been cut, place them together in a row in the vice and trim again with the spokeshave until the curves match for all four lengths.

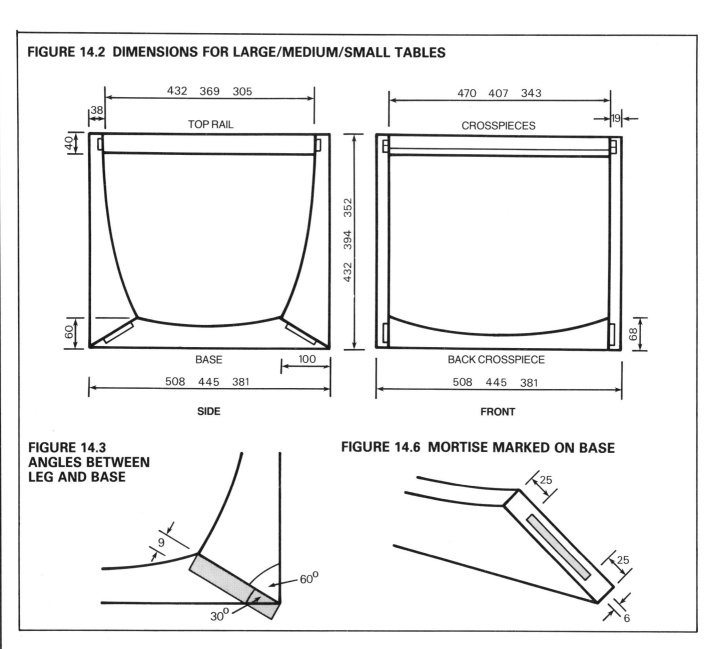

FIGURE 14.2 DIMENSIONS FOR LARGE/MEDIUM/SMALL TABLES

TOP RAIL
432 369 305
38
40

CROSSPIECES
470 407 343
19

432 394 352

BASE
508 445 381
60
100

SIDE

BACK CROSSPIECE
508 445 381
68

FRONT

FIGURE 14.3 ANGLES BETWEEN LEG AND BASE

9
60°
30°

FIGURE 14.6 MORTISE MARKED ON BASE

25
25
6

FIGURE 14.4

FIGURE 14.5

6 Next, prepare the two bases, cutting straight along the 30° mortise lines and planing flat. Once again, line up the pieces to check for consistency in the curve. Lastly, cut out the curved back crosspiece.

7 The mortise and tenon joints are now ready to be cut for the base and legs. Set the mortise gauge markers to a gap of 6 mm and adjust the fence so that they scribe the wood centrally on its 19 mm-thick edge. Score the lines on the mortise faces of the base and then set in each mortise by 25 mm from each end (Figure 14.6).

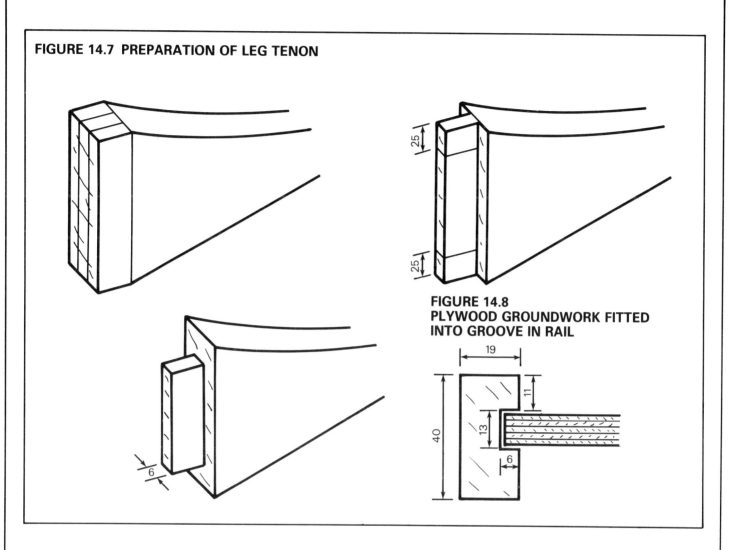

FIGURE 14.7 PREPARATION OF LEG TENON

FIGURE 14.8 PLYWOOD GROUNDWORK FITTED INTO GROOVE IN RAIL

8 Clamp the piece securely in the vice and chop out the mortises with the 6 mm chisel and mallet. Chisel with care to make sure that the wood does not split beneath the mortise where it tapers towards the pointed end. A depth gauge set to 9 mm should be used to check when sufficient wood has been chopped out.

9 Mark the tenon at the bottom of each leg, using the mortise gauge at the same setting. Then clamp the wood in the vice and remove the shoulders with the tenon saw. Set in the tenon by a matching 25 mm from each end and saw off the remaining two shoulders (Figure 14.7).

10 Fit the joint together experimentally, trimming off any excess wood until the leg fits tightly up against the base.

11 When all four mortise and tenon joints are complete for the two bases and four legs, prepare smaller four-shouldered mortise and tenons to fit the top side rails. The rail width is 40 mm, so mark this at the top of all four legs and score the mortise lines with the gauge on the same setting as that used previously. Set in the shoulders by 9 mm at the top and 3 mm at the bottom. Chop out the mortises to a depth of 9 mm.

12 If the spokeshave has put a noticeable curve on the face of the mortise, plane it flat with the 19 mm chisel. Before cutting the top rail to length, check it with the tape as it might be slightly different from the measurement shown in Figure 14.2, due to trimming.

13 Mark in the tenons at both ends of each rail and saw off the shoulders in the usual way. Fit the joints together one at a time, and when each one slots fully home, temporarily assemble the whole side comprising the base, two legs and top rail. Check that both side sections of the table are identical.

14 Dismantle them again and mark out the housing groove on the inside face of both side rails using the mortise gauge set to a gap of 13 mm and with the fence adjusted to 11 mm. Cut the groove along the entire length of the rail with the plough plane, working it to a depth of 6 mm. This will later accommodate the plywood groundwork (Figure 14.8).

15 Mix a quantity of wood glue and assemble each side section one at a

FIGURE 14.9 RAIL AND LEG

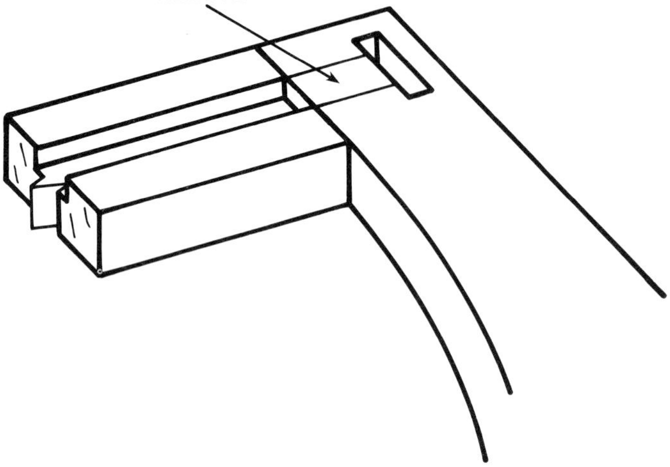

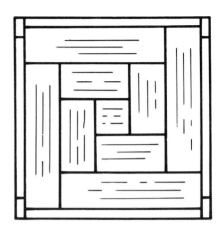

REMOVE

FIGURE 14.11 WOODBLOCK PATTERN FOR TABLE TOP

time. Tap the joints together and when the assembly is complete, cramp it up tightly and wipe away any excess glue from the joints with a damp rag. Place to one side for a day.

16 When the glue has set hard, remove the cramps and rub down the surfaces with medium and then fine-grade sandpaper.

17 To complete the table frame, both side sections must now be joined together with three crosspieces (Figure 14.2). The first of these is the curved crosspiece, fitted along the bottom of the table at the back. The other two fit at the top: the one that goes at the back is 40 mm wide, and the one at the front is 28 mm. As explained earlier, the front rail is narrower to permit the medium and small tables to stow away inside the large table. Only the small table has the full-width 40 mm rail both front and back. If you are making one table only, rather than a set of three, make a second curved crosspiece for the bottom and fit it at the front.

18 Fit the bottom crosspiece(s) using the mortise and tenon joint as

before, setting in the secondary shoulders by 10 mm top and bottom. Mark and cut mortise and tenons for the two top rails, varying the size of the joint to suit the differing widths of the rails.

19 When all the crosspieces fit into position, stand the table on a flat surface to check for overall squareness.

20 Dismantle the crosspieces and mark the two top crosspieces on their inside faces with housing joint grooves as you did previously for the side rails, removing the waste with the plough plane to a depth of 6 mm. Using the 6 mm chisel, extend the grooves in the side sections across the legs so that they meet the mortises (Figure 14.9).

21 Cut the table top plywood groundwork to size and slot it into the grooves, assembling the table experimentally to check that it all fits tightly together.

22 Mix more wood glue, brush it well into the grooves and joints, and knock the table together (Figure

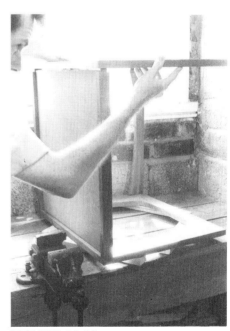

FIGURE 14.10

14.10), cramping up the joints and wiping away surplus glue.

23 When the glue has set hard, rub down the table thoroughly with medium and fine-grade sandpaper, rounding off all the edges and corners.

24 Cut the woodblocks to size, following the dimensions given in the cutting list depending on which size of table you are making. Mark the blocks or tiles to length with the square and pencil, then cut it up with the tenon saw and plane the ends to form perfect right-angles.

25 Starting with the outermost row, fit the woodblocks in position one by one. After completing the row, work inwards with the middle row next, finishing with the single centre block (Figures 14.11 and 14.12). Number each tile so that it can be put back later in the same position.

26 Remove all the tiles, then apply a strong adhesive over the surface of the groundwork. Lay the tiles in place, applying glue to their edges. Tap them gently down to allow surplus adhesive to squeeze out, preventing an air pocket from being trapped beneath.

27 When all the woodblocks are in position, wipe away excess glue from

FIGURE 14.12

the top surface, and cover it with a sheet of paper, placing a heavy weight on top to keep the blocks under pressure as the glue sets hard.

28 After a day or so, rub down the top surface with fine sandpaper and keep rubbing until the surface is absolutely flat and smooth. Because the woodblock tiles are 9 mm thick and the recess is 11 mm deep from the top of the frame to the plywood

groundwork, the tiles are inset by 2 mm into the table.

29 The table may have two different types of finish, depending on choice. The frame is best given several applications of teak oil or Danish oil, which gives the sides and the rails a pleasant dark stain and brings out the grain. When the oil has dried thoroughly, the surfaces should be rubbed over with a good wax polish. The table top, being more susceptible during years of use to knocks and spillages of drink, should be coated with several layers of semi-matt polyurethane varnish. Between each coat, when it has dried out, rub down the surface with fine sandpaper to remove blemishes such as tiny air bubbles.

30 Finally, fix four small round-headed brass tacks into the underside of the base, one in each corner. These are at 10 mm diameter and act as substitutes for the larger 'domes of silence' often found beneath items of furniture.

questions

(a) Why are templates used (Paragraphs 1, 2 and 3), instead of simply marking the curves directly on the wood?

(b) In Paragraph 8, what is the best way of safeguarding against the chisel splitting the wood under the mortise where it tapers towards the pointed end?

(c) Why is it very important to mark and cut the housing groove in the two side rails (Paragraph 14) before the side section is assembled?

(d) What is the purpose of the table top groundwork (Paragraph 21)? Why is plywood the most suitable material for it?

exercises

(i) Using the same basic design, adapt it to produce a long john table, which is a rectangular low table where the length is at least double the width.

(ii) Redesign the joint between the base and the legs to give an angle of 45° each instead of 30° and 60° in our design. How does this affect the curvature of the legs and base?

(iii) Suggest an alternative woodblock pattern for the top surface. If necessary, you may use different sizes of woodblock tile.

(iv) Design your own set of coffee tables, using straight rather than curved legs. Consider turning the legs on the lathe to produce your own decorative patterns.

(v) Work out the cost of making the coffee tables using different types of wood, such as the alternatives like Burmese teak, agba and Brazilian mahogany already mentioned.

project 15
the passageway door

A door that is used for an outside passageway, or the garage or garden shed, is often of the framed-and-braced variety. It is a very strong type of door, and provided it is treated with a water repellent preservative, it should last for many years. Most exterior doors rot away in time, and therefore you may want to make a replacement.

how it is designed

Though it might look complicated, the framed-and-braced door is quite a straightforward structure, provided that you measure accurately.

Its components are the two upright stiles; the top, mid and bottom rails; two diagonal braces one of which runs between the top and mid rails, the other between the mid and bottom rails; and lastly the V-edged tongued and grooved matchboarding which covers the frame (Figure 15.2).

The braces are not there for decoration — they both have the important function of giving increased strength to the structure, in the same way that a gate is often braced (see Project 16). The braces are always arranged with the lower end fitted to the hinging stile.

The two stiles and the top rail are all rebated to the thickness of the matchboarding. The mid and bottom rails and the braces, however, are less thick and lie flush with the rebates.

The main joints are through-and-wedged mortise and tenons, used to secure the rails to the stiles. The braces are tongued at the ends, and fit into slots cut in the rails and stiles. The matchboarding slots together and fits into the rebated section of the framework (Figure 15.3), being fixed in position with nails.

You will notice that the mid and bottom rails are both much wider

than the top rail, and they have double tenons which help to counteract the effects of wood shrinkage.

The timber is red deal.

tool list

Pencil
ruler
square
mortise gauge
tenon saw
handsaw
16 mm bevel chisel
mallet
handbrace with 13 mm centre bit
plane
plough plane
hammer
file

FIGURE 15.1

cutting list

Item	Long mm	Wide mm	Thick mm
2 stiles	1980	96	48
1 top rail	740 (548)	96	48
1 mid rail	740 (548)	140	29
1 bottom rail	740 (548)	146	29
2 braces	1000	96	29
7 lengths of matchboarding	1898	100	19

Note: The figures in brackets above refer to rail lengths minus tenons.

The two stiles and the top rail all have 19 mm-deep rebates cut into one face.

how to make it

1 Prepare the rebates in the stiles and the top rail, using the plough plane. The rebates measure 19 mm in depth and 12 mm in width (Figure 15.3).

2 Place the stiles side by side on a flat surface. Measure and mark the mortises for each rail, using the steel tape measure, pencil and square. Square the pencil lines across the two stiles, and continue marking the lines right around both pieces. Before cutting the stiles to length, allow an excess of wood at both ends — this will be trimmed at a later stage, but for the moment it helps to prevent the top and bottom mortises from splitting the wood as they are being cut.

3 Mark in the mortises. Following the rule that the mortise should equal one-third the thickness of the wood, set the pointers of the gauge to the width of the 16 mm chisel. But only in the case of the top rail is the mortise absolutely central — its normal position. For the mid and bottom rails it must be marked in level with the rebate. Adjust the fence of the gauge to mark the stile in the required position. Since each mortise is to be cut right through, turn the stile over and mark the opposite side as well.

4 Set in the mortise to allow for the shoulders of the rail tenons. The top rail is set in by 32 mm at the top and 12 mm at the bottom to lie flush with the rebate. The mid rail is set in by 6 mm top and bottom, and the bottom rail by 6 mm for the top and 13 mm for the bottom.

5 The mid and bottom mortises are split up into thirds to create the accommodation for double tenons.

6 Finally mark an extra 6 mm at the top and bottom of each mortise on the outer face of the stile so that a sloped portion may be cut out to take the wedges used during assembly (Figure 15.4).

7 Taking the first stile, clamp it in the vice with a suitable support and

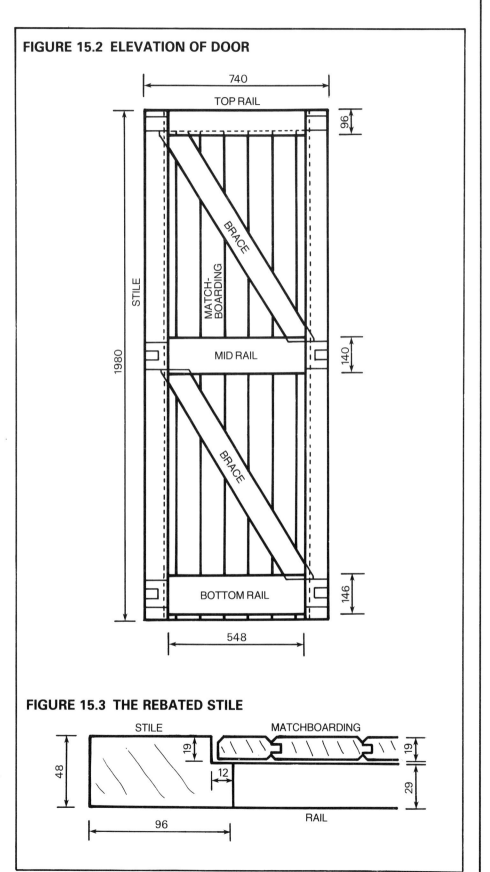

FIGURE 15.2 ELEVATION OF DOOR

FIGURE 15.3 THE REBATED STILE

FIGURE 15.4 THE WEDGED THROUGH MORTISE AND TENON

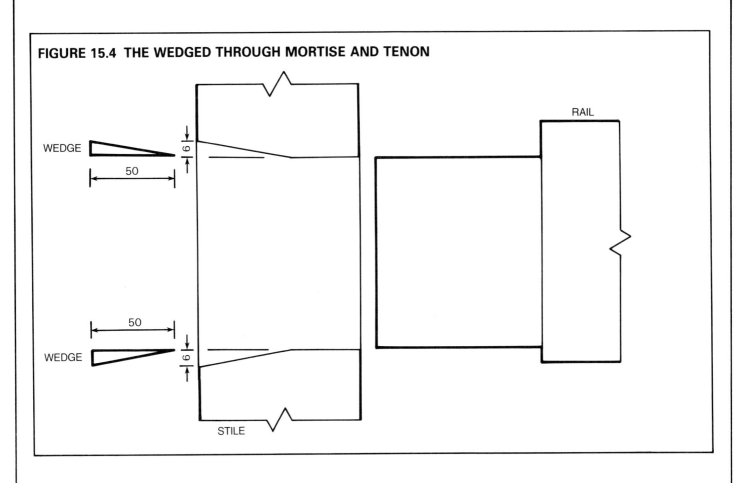

WEDGE

50

6

WEDGE

50

6

STILE

RAIL

FIGURE 15.5

chop out the mortises. This is best done in two stages. Begin by drilling out the waste using the 13 mm centre bit fitted in the handbrace. The drill is slightly smaller in diameter than the width of the mortise. Bore out a series of holes halfway through the wood, then turn the piece over and start again from the opposite side until the holes meet. This gets rid of most of the waste quickly and easily. Finish by chopping out the remaining waste with the 16 mm chisel (Figure 15.5).

8 When all six mortises have been cut, measure for the tenons in the corresponding rails. Taking each rail in turn, mark in the shoulders of the two tenons, each of which is equal in depth to the 96 mm width of the stile. Complete the marking of the tenon by scoring the two parallel lines with the mortise gauge, matching this to the exact width of the mortise and remembering that the top mortise only is located centrally in the stile.

9 The tenons for the mid and bottom rails are slightly different, due to the fact that the rails lie flush with the rebates. They are called bare-faced tenons, having only one main shoulder cut instead of the usual two. The other difference is that they are double tenons, with a rectangular portion cut out to match precisely with the wood that remains in the centre of the mortise.

10 Starting with the top rail (Figure 15.6), noting the long and

short shoulders, place the piece in the vice and cut the tenons. The shoulders are removed in the usual way, with the tenon saw. Measure and cut the remaining two shoulders that set in the tenon to match the mortise, and finally trim the tenon to fit the rebate. File both the mortise and tenon to obtain a smooth easy fit.

11 For the bare-faced tenons of the mid and bottom rails (Figure 15.7), cut away a shoulder on one side only. Then carefully measure out the rectangular portion for the double tenon and remove the waste using the tenon saw and chisel.

12 When all the joints are complete, assemble the framework loosely to check that all three rails fit fully into the stiles. In particular, check for overall squareness at every corner.

13 The next step is to measure the braces. Lay the framework on a flat surface and position the two lengths

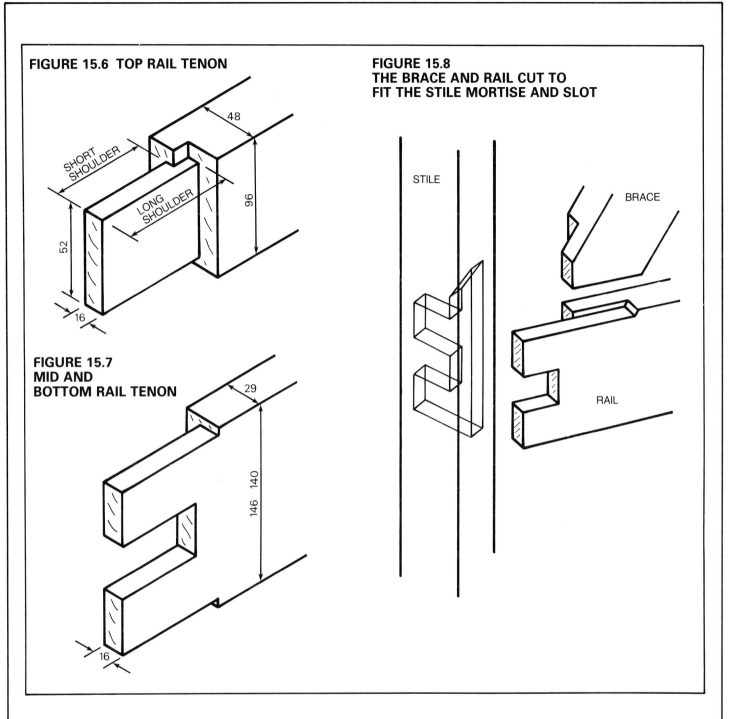

FIGURE 15.6 TOP RAIL TENON

SHORT SHOULDER

LONG SHOULDER

48

96

52

16

**FIGURE 15.7
MID AND
BOTTOM RAIL TENON**

29

146   140

16

**FIGURE 15.8
THE BRACE AND RAIL CUT TO
FIT THE STILE MORTISE AND SLOT**

STILE

BRACE

RAIL

of brace material across both diagonals, as in Figure 15.2. A slot must now be cut in the rail and stile to receive a tongue sawn at the two ends of each brace. Figure 15.8 illustrates that the stile slot is simply a continuation of the mortise, except that its depth is only 25 mm. A narrow channel is cut in the rail to take the brace likewise.

14 Measure and cut the brace to size, allowing for the tongues being set 25 mm into the stiles and 6 mm into the rails. Then re-position the brace over the framework and mark in the depths of each slot to be cut in the rail and stile, together with the angle at which the brace meets them. Use the mortise gauge to mark in the slots, and chop out the waste with the chisel, leaving the stile as in Figure 15.9.

FIGURE 15.9

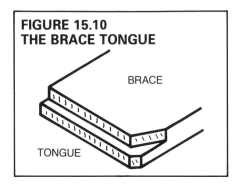

**FIGURE 15.10
THE BRACE TONGUE**

BRACE

TONGUE

15   Use the same mortise gauge setting to mark out the tongues, and cut these to size (Figure 15.10). The method is the same as cutting the bare-faced tenons.

16   Assemble the framework again, this time with the braces which should fit snugly into position (Figure 15.11). You may need to tap the joints together quite hard, using the mallet and a block of scrap wood. If all is well, dismantle the frame and treat with wood preservative, especially in the joints. This takes several days to dry thoroughly.

17   The framework is now ready for final assembly, using wood glue and hardwood wedges. There are twenty wedges in all, and these should measure approximately 50 mm in length, 16 mm in width and 6 mm in

FIGURE 15.11

thickness at the maximum point of the wedge (Figure 15.4).

18   Mix a quantity of wood glue and apply it with a brush to each of the

joints on one side, securing the rails and braces to the stile. Repeat for the other stile, and drive it home with the mallet. Cramp up the framework, then start tapping in the wedges after brushing them thoroughly with glue. Take care not to hit them too hard, or you will risk splitting the wood. Wipe away excess glue with a damp rag, and allow at least a day for the joints to set hard.

19   The V-edged tongued and grooved matchboarding can now be arranged for fitting. It is highly unlikely that its several boards can be slotted together and dropped straight into position — the outer boards will need trimming to size. Measure how much waste should be removed from each, mark this in with a pencil line and plane off the unwanted wood, working a fresh V-edge. By treating the two outermost boards equally, the result will be well-balanced to the eye.

20   Give the boards a thorough treatment with preservative, especially in the grooves, and when dry, nail the boards in position with 38 mm oval-headed wire nails. These should be hammered down in pairs, in a dovetail pattern for increased strength. Trim the matchboarding at the bottom of the door, and apply more preservative.

questions

(a)   The braces are an important part of the design of the door, and you are told to fit them with their lower ends in the hinging stile. Why? And what would happen if you got this wrong?

(b)   Why do double tenons help to counteract the effects of wood shrinkage?

(c)   You can prepare the mortises more quickly by removing much of the waste with the drill (Paragraph 7). There is one disadvantage in using this method. Explain what this is, and why it is so.

(d)   Why does the top rail have tenons with long and short shoulders?

(e)   Why do the wedges make for more secure mortise and tenon joints?

(f)   In fixing the matchboarding to the frame (Paragraph 20), why is it that when the nails are hammered down in pairs in a dovetail pattern this gives extra strength to the assembly?

exercises

(i)   It is quite likely that you would have to make a door that is either slightly wider or narrower than our example. Using the same basic framework and the same sections of timber, calculate the new rail and brace lengths and the amount of matchboarding required to fit your own particular door frame.

(ii)   Hanging a door accurately is quite difficult, and needs a lot of care. Describe how you would set about it, and ask yourself these questions: what hinges do I use; how many hinges should this door have; which way around do I fit them; how do I make the rebates for the hinges; what type of latch should I fit?

project 16
the driveway gates

A pair of traditional wooden driveway gates still has great appeal, particularly when they are stained a natural colour to show the grain. When constructed with diagonal braces, the gates possess sufficient strength to withstand many years' use. The wood will last for a long time if it is treated with a water-repellent preservative. Like the door in the previous project, gates inevitably rot away in time, and you might want to build a replacement pair.

FIGURE 16.1

how they are designed

In most respects, the driveway gates are similar to the passageway door. They each have a braced framework, the lower part of which is rebated to house tongued and grooved matchboarding.

The parts that make up each gate are the two upright stiles; the top, mid and bottom rails; a diagonal brace; four bars and ten lengths of V-edged matchboarding (Figure 16.2).

The brace has the important function of giving increased strength to the structure, in the same way that the passageway door was braced (see Project 15). The brace is always arranged with its lower end fitted to the hinging stile — that is, the outer stile which rests adjacent to the gatepost. With double gates, the appearance of the two braces will be that of an inverted V.

The mid and bottom rails are rebated to the thickness of the matchboarding. The brace is less thick and lies flush with the rebates.

The main joints are through-and-wedged mortise and tenons, used to secure the rails to the stiles. The braces are tongued at the ends, and

fit into grooves cut in the rails and stiles. The bars are fitted with stopped mortise and tenons, and the matchboarding slots together and is housed in grooves cut in both the mid and bottom rails.

The timber used in the illustrated example is Western red cedar, which is a comparatively light softwood ideally suited to this sort of use, since gates have to stand up to all weathers. You could use red deal, but this will make the finished gates much heavier, as would using a hardwood like oak. To counteract the additional weight, you should make the gates thinner, 45 mm instead of 57 mm.

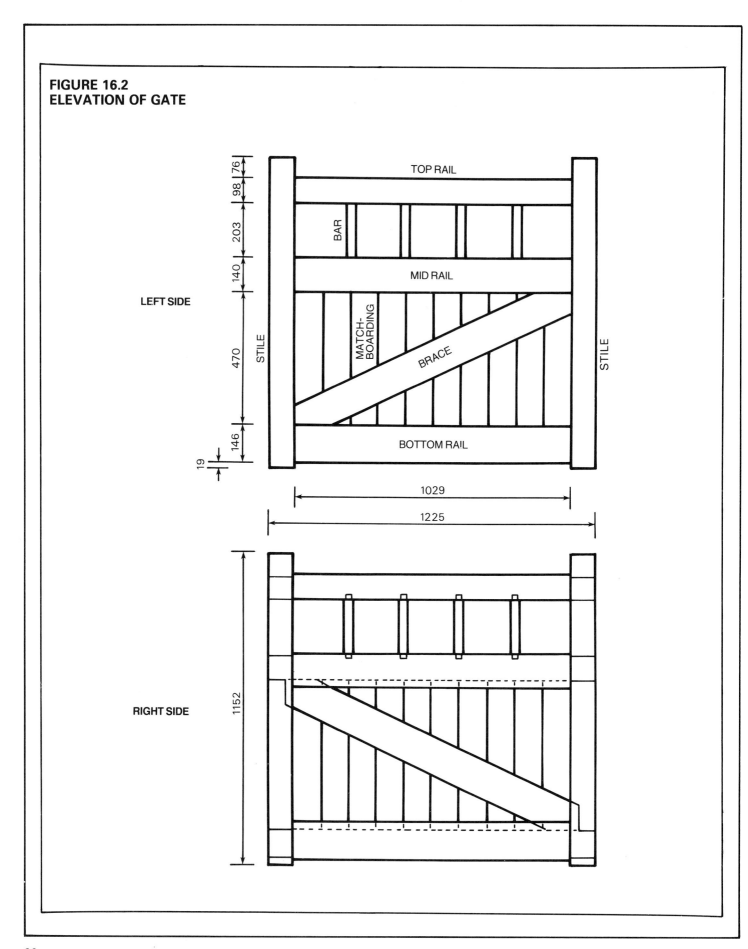

FIGURE 16.2
ELEVATION OF GATE

LEFT SIDE

TOP RAIL

BAR

MID RAIL

MATCH-BOARDING

BRACE

STILE

STILE

BOTTOM RAIL

76
98
203
140
470
146
19

1029

1225

RIGHT SIDE

1152

tool list

Pencil
ruler
square
mortise gauge
tenon saw
handsaw
19 mm bevel chisel
mallet
handbrace with 16 mm centre bit
plane
plough plane
file

cutting list

Item	Long mm	Wide mm	Thick mm
4 stiles	1152	98	57
2 top rails	1225 (1029)	98	57
2 mid rails	1225 (1029)	140	57
2 bottom rails	1225 (1029)	146	57
2 braces	1200 (1150)	140	38
8 bars	229 (203)	44	44
20 lengths of matchboarding	534 (508)	110	17

Note: The figures in brackets above refer to lengths minus tenons.

The mid and bottom rails both have 19 mm-square rebates cut into one edge.

how to make them

1 Prepare the rebates in the mid and bottom rails, using the plough plane. The rebates measure 19 mm square.

2 Place the four stiles side by side on a flat surface. Allowing an excess of wood at both ends, measure and mark the mortises for each rail, using a steel tape measure, pencil and square. Square the pencil lines across all four stiles, and continue marking the lines right around each individual piece.

3 Mark in the mortises. Following the rule that the mortise should equal one-third the thickness of the wood, set the pointers of the gauge to the width of the 19 mm chisel. Since the mortise is to be cut right through, turn the stile over and mark the opposite side as well.

4 Set in each mortise to allow for the shoulders of the rail tenons. The top rail is set in by 6 mm at the top only. The mid rail is set in by 6 mm at the top and 19 mm at the bottom, where it lines up precisely with the rebate. The bottom rail is an exact reverse, with 19 mm at the top and 6 mm at the bottom.

5 Finally mark an extra 6 mm at the top and bottom of each mortise on the outer face of the stile so that a sloped portion may be cut out for wedges to be fitted into the joints during assembly (Figure 16.3).

6 Taking the first stile, clamp it in the vice with a suitable support and chop out the mortises. This is best done in two stages. Begin by drilling out the waste using the 16 mm centre bit fitted to the handbrace. The drill is slightly smaller in diameter than the width of the mortise. Bore out a series of holes halfway through the wood, then turn the piece over and start again from the opposite side until the holes meet and pass right through the stile. This gets rid of most of the waste quickly and easily.

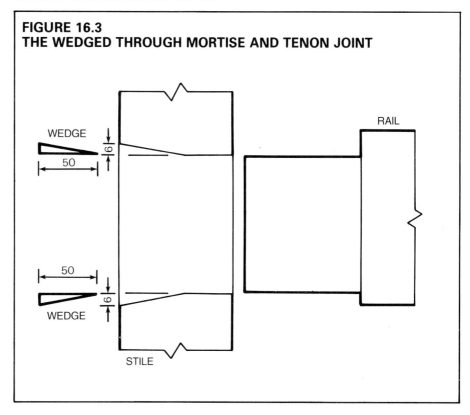

FIGURE 16.3
THE WEDGED THROUGH MORTISE AND TENON JOINT

WEDGE
50
6

WEDGE
50
6

STILE

RAIL

FIGURE 16.4

7 Finish the mortise by chopping out the remaining waste with the 19mm chisel (Figure 16.4), cutting cleanly into the wood to give a neat result. Take care when trimming close up to the line, however, because cedar has a tendency to break off in small clumps when struck with the chisel across the grain.

8 When all twelve mortises have been chopped out satisfactorily,

measure for the tenons in the corresponding rails. Taking each rail in turn, mark in the shoulders of the two tenons, each of which is equal in length to the width of the stile. Complete the marking of the tenon by scoring the two parallel lines with the mortise gauge, matching this to the exact width of the mortise.

9 Prepare the tenons with the rail held securely in the vice. Due to the fact that the ordinary tenon saw will only cut to a limited depth, it will be necessary to use the handsaw for much of the work. When the two main shoulders have been removed, measure and cut the remaining two shoulders — in the case of the top rail, the one remaining shoulder (Figure 16.5) — that set in the tenon to match the mortise. Test the joint for a smooth fit. If it binds at all, file down any irregularity.

10 When all the mortises and tenons are complete, the bare

framework of the gate can be loosely assembled to check that all three rails fit fully into the stiles. In particular, check for overall squareness before proceeding from this point.

11 The next step is to measure the brace. Lay the framework of the gate on a flat surface and position the length of brace material across the diagonal, as in Figure 16.2. A slot must now be cut in the rail and stile to receive a tongue sawn at both ends of the brace.

12 Figure 16.6 illustrates that the stile slot is simply a continuation of the mortise, except that its depth is only 25mm. A narrow channel is cut likewise in the rail. As the rebate in both mid and bottom rails is designed to house the matchboarding, the brace is mounted on the fullest portion of the rail, leaving the rebate free.

13 Measure and cut the brace to size, allowing for the tongues being set

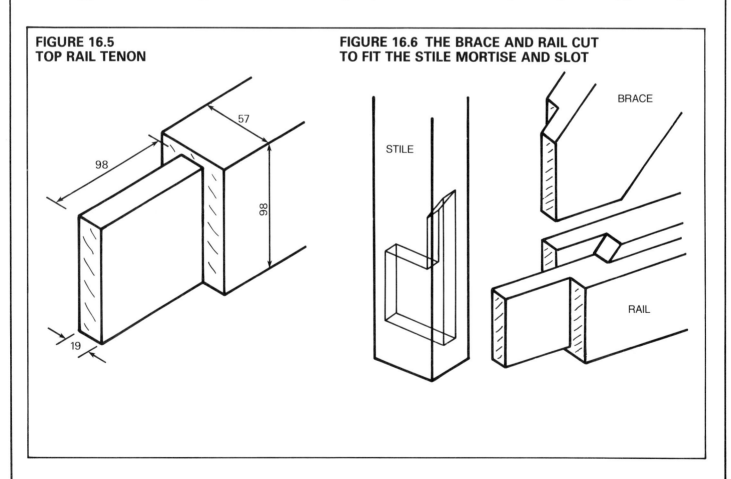

FIGURE 16.5
TOP RAIL TENON

FIGURE 16.6 THE BRACE AND RAIL CUT TO FIT THE STILE MORTISE AND SLOT

STILE

BRACE

RAIL

FIGURE 16.7

25 mm into the stiles and 19 mm into the rails. Then re-position the brace over the framework of the gate (Figure 16.7), and mark in the depths of each slot to be cut in the rail and stile, together with the angle at which the brace meets them. Use the mortise gauge to mark in the slots, and chop out the waste with the chisel.

14 Use the same mortise gauge setting to mark out the tongues at either end of the brace, and cut these out (Figure 16.8).

15 Assemble the framework again, this time with the braces which should fit snugly into position (Figure 16.9).

FIGURE 16.9

16 The next step is to cut and fit the four bars in each gate. These are spaced at equal intervals between the top and mid rails. Once again, the mortise and tenon is used, this one being of the stopped variety. The mortise is cut 32 mm square and 13 mm deep, the tenon having four 6 mm-thick shoulders. Prepare all eight joints in the usual way, checking that they fit together satisfactorily (Figure 16.10).

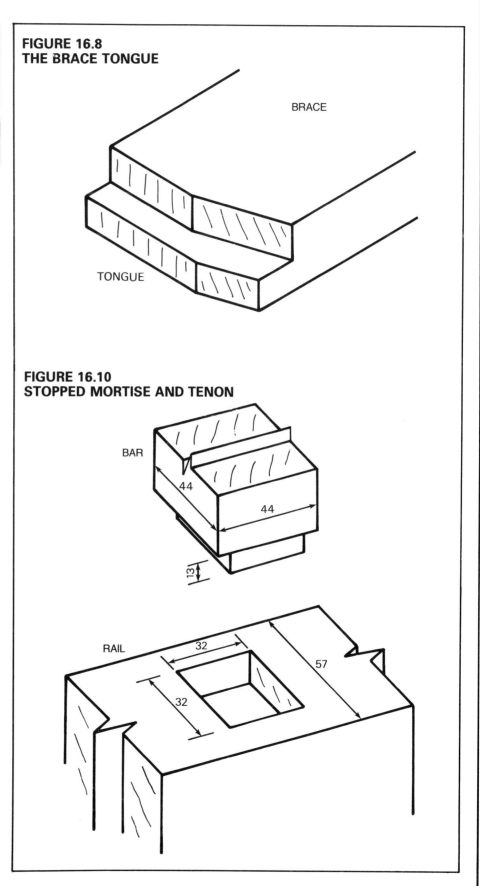

**FIGURE 16.8
THE BRACE TONGUE**

BRACE

TONGUE

**FIGURE 16.10
STOPPED MORTISE AND TENON**

BAR

44

44

13

RAIL

32

32

57

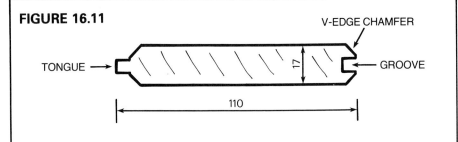

FIGURE 16.11

TONGUE →

V-EDGE CHAMFER

← GROOVE

17

110

FIGURE 16.12
REBATED, GROOVED AND CHAMFERED RAILS

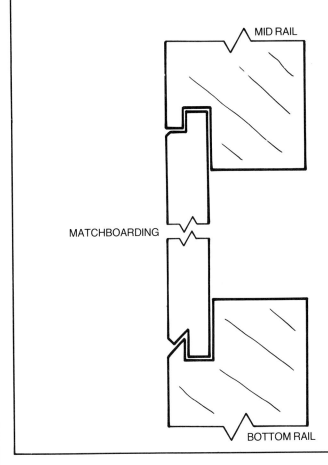

MID RAIL

MATCHBOARDING

BOTTOM RAIL

19 When the grooves have been cut in the mid and bottom rails, finish off the bottom one by planing a sloped ledge on the rebate so that when rain water runs down the boarding it will tend to drip onto the rail and then drain off. There is no need to do this to the mid rail.

20 Measure out each individual length of matchboarding, allowing for the 13 mm tongue required at either end to fit into the rebate grooves. Cut to length and then mark in the tongues, bearing in mind that the top tongue is a straightforward right-angled cross-cut, whilst the bottom tongue is angled inwards and upwards to copy the direction of the sloped ledge on the bottom rail (Figure 16.12). Cut out the tongues.

21 Arrange the matchboarding in position between the mid and bottom rails. It is highly unlikely that the ten boards will fit exactly — the outer boards will probably need trimming to size. Plane off the unwanted wood, and finish off by planing a fresh chamfer. By treating the two outermost boards equally, the result will be well-balanced to the eye.

22 Give all the components a thorough treatment with preservative, especially in the grooves and joints. When dry, the gates are ready for final assembly.

23 The gates are assembled using wood glue and hardwood wedges. There are twenty-four wedges in all for the two gates, and these should measure approximately 50 mm in length, 19 mm in width and 6 mm in thickness at the maximum point of the wedge (Figure 16.3).

17 The final part of the gates is the matchboarding. If you are using Western red cedar, plane the wood to size and cut the tongues and grooves with the plough plane, using the appropriate cutters. Chamfer the V-edge, using the plane. A cross-section is shown in Figure 16.11.

18 The method of fixing the matchboarding into position between the mid and bottom rails is illustrated in Figure 16.12. A groove half the thickness of the matchboarding material is cut along the innermost section of the rebate to a depth of 13 mm, using the plough plane (Figure 16.13). As the total thickness of the matchboarding is slightly less than that of the rebate, it will be set in fractionally, rather than lying flush with the rails and stiles.

FIGURE 16.13

24 Glue the bars into place between the top and mid rails, then glue both rails into one stile. Fit the bottom rail and the brace. Glue the grooves for the matchboarding and slide these one by one into position, in the desired order. Finally glue the second stile and tap this down, knocking all the joints fully home.

25 Brush each of the wedges with glue and drive them into their slots with the mallet. Guard against trying to force them in too hard, or you will risk splitting the wood. Wipe away excess glue with a damp rag, and allow at least a day for the joints to set hard. Trim the stiles to their true length.

26 Galvanised nails may be used to fix the matchboarding more securely to the brace.

27 Rub down the surfaces with fine sandpaper, and apply more preservative. Cedar is an absorbent wood, and several coats will be necessary.

questions

(a) As in the previous project, the braces are an important part of the design of the gates, and you are told to fit them with their lower ends in the hinging stile. Why? And what would happen if you fitted them the wrong way?

(b) You can prepare the mortises more quickly by removing much of the waste with the drill (Paragraph 6). There is one disadvantage in using this method, particularly with a wood like red cedar. Explain what this is, and why it is so.

(c) Gates, like any outdoor woodwork, will get wet often. What effect does this have on the wood? How can you offset the effect? Do you see any particular feature in the gates to suggest that this is allowed for?

exercises

(i) Adapt the design of the driveway gates to suit a single narrow pathway gate, retaining the brace.

(ii) Work out the difference in cost between making the driveway gates in Western red cedar and red deal, and compare these both with the cost of using a hardwood like oak. Explore the possibility of cheaper hardwoods, remembering that they must withstand years of weathering.

(iii) As in the case of the passageway door (Project 15), hanging a pair of gates accurately is difficult, and needs great care. Bearing in mind that the illustrated example uses standard-size double-strap hinges, describe how you would set about the task, and ask yourself these questions: what hinges and hinge-pins do I use; where on the gates should the hinges go; how do I best take up any gap between the hinges and the wood of the gates; what type of latch should I fit?

tool list

Most of the tools used in this book are illustrated and described below.

square — also known by its full name **try-square** — this has a wooden handle and a flat metal blade set at 90° to one another, to mark lines perpendicularly across the wood.

marking gauge and **mortise gauge** — two similar tools used for scribing straight lines on the wood with either one or two metal pointers. The marking gauge has one pointer, and the mortise gauge (shown) has two, the second of which is adjustable by turning a small knob at the end of the shaft. In both cases there is also a sliding fence used to set the desired position of the pointer(s).

tenon saw — a fine-toothed saw with a reinforced top edge used for cutting tenons, and most other joints requiring precision.

handsaw — larger than the tenon saw and more flexible, with a choice of cross-cut or ripping teeth, depending on the type of work it is to do. A very useful saw for cutting large sections of wood quickly and easily.

hacksaw — the illustrated example is a junior hacksaw, which has an extremely fine-toothed replaceable blade secured to a metal frame, making this a useful tool for cutting small pieces of wood and metal.

coping saw — this has a narrower blade than the hacksaw, and the metal frame has a deeper back. The blade can be turned within the frame, allowing this saw to cut curved lines.

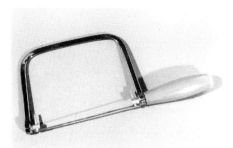

bevel chisel — a good general-purpose wood chisel available in a variety of widths. The bevel is essential for chopping out dovetails, the other type of chisel without the bevel being called the firmer chisel. There is also a tool called a mortise chisel, which has a stronger blade capable of withstanding considerable leverage.

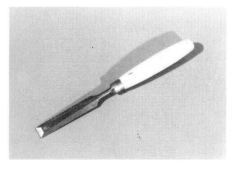

mallet — a wooden hammer usually with a large ash head and a beech shaft, used for striking the chisel.

brace — a crank-handled drill used for boring holes. Shown with it are a centre-bit and twist drill.

smoothing plane — probably the most useful size of plane, this is the handtool which turns a rough surface into a smooth finish, or reduces the width or thickness of a piece of wood. The blade should always be kept very sharp, and retracted when the plane is not in use. Never lay the plane flat on the workbench if the blade is in the working position, but prop it in the tooltray so that the sharp cutting edge does not come into contact with any surface.

spokeshave — this is the metal-handled variety, though wooden-handled spokeshaves are available. It is used for planing curved surfaces, and some skill is required to work it well.

bradawl — a pointed instrument for marking holes before drilling. Some bradawls have squared pointed tips.

file — a flat file for removing small amounts of waste from flat surfaces, such as a slightly oversize tenon.

trimming knife — a sharp-bladed knife with a good firm handle for marking and trimming.

hammer — the illustrated example is a claw-hammer — for driving home nails. Other hammer patterns are available, such as the ballpein and crosspein.

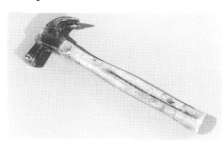

screwdriver — this one has a big round wooden handle which makes it easy to grasp and a long shaft giving it a good reach.

plough plane — a specialist tool used to cut rebates, grooves, fillets, and other pieces of work. Though the electric rebater has to a large extent replaced the traditional plough plane, this is a useful tool and one with which the woodworker should be proficient.

parting tool, skew chisel and spindle gouge — three handtools designed for woodturning and used in conjunction with the lathe.

mitre box — a box, usually made of beech or some similar hardwood, with 45° and 90° angles already cut in its sides to take a saw blade and guide it so that it will cut accurate mitres.

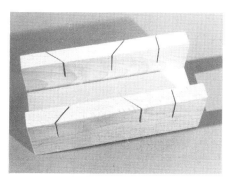

tool and material manufacturers and suppliers

Planes, chisels, saws and hammers

E.J. Arnold and Sons Ltd, Butterley Street, Leeds, LS10 1AX

Record Ridgway Tools Ltd, Parkway Works, Sheffield, S9 3BL

Stanley Tools Ltd, Woodside, Sheffield, S3 9PD

Cramps

John Burn & Co (B'ham) Ltd, 74 Albert Road, Stechford, Birmingham B33 9AJ

Record Ridgway Tools Ltd, Parkway Works, Sheffield, S9 3BL

Portable power tools

Buck and Ryan Ltd, 101 Tottenham Court Road, London W1

Heward and Dean Ltd, 90/94 West Green Road, London N15 4SR

Stanley Bridges Ltd, Nelson Way, Cramlington, Newcastle-on-Tyne

Circular saw benches

Startrite Machine Tool Co Ltd, 69-71 Newington Causeway, London SE1

Lathes

Spear and Jackson (Tools) Ltd, St Paul's Road, Wednesbury, Staffordshire, WS10 9RA

Hard and soft woods

John Boddy and Sons (Timber) Ltd, Riverside Sawmills, Boroughbridge, North Yorkshire, YO5 9LJ

Fitchett and Woollacott Ltd, Willow Road, Lenton Lane, Nottingham, NG7 2PR

S. Silverman and Son (Importers) Ltd, Chilton Street, London E2 6EA

Solarbo Ltd, Commerce Way, Lancing, Sussex

Adhesives

Borden (UK) Ltd, North Baddesley, Southampton, SO5 9ZB

Ciba-Geigy (UK) Ltd, Plastics Division, Duxford, Cambridge, CB2 4QA

Gloy, Eighth Avenue, Manor Park, London, E12 5JW

The names and addresses listed under all the above headings are only a selection of the many firms supplying tools and materials for woodworking purposes. You would be well advised to consult a directory for your own local area to find out if there is a manufacturer or supplier who has not been listed here.